Conversations For Action and Collected Essays

Instilling A Culture of Commitment in Working Relationships

By

Dr. Fernando Flores

Edited by

Maria Flores Letelier

ISBN: 1478378484

ISBN 13: 9781478378488

Library of Congress Control Number: 2012914423
CreateSpace Independent Publishing Platform
North Charleston, South Carolina

For Gloria, wife, mother and inspiration

Table of Contents

Foreward

At long last, here is a volume of the Fernando Flores' original essays on his philosophy of communication, which has become so important in business. Bravo!

Many of these essays circulated in an underground of Fernando's students and business clients, but did not see the light of day or become available as a collection. Until now. Finally all those who asked for such a collection will be satisfied. Although written in the 1980s, there is a timelessness about the essays: they speak vividly to issues we encounter today.

I especially like the commentary by Fernando at the beginning. It gives a nice summary, in his own words, of the key ideas in his thought. It also explains the inspirations behind the ideas.

I also liked the introduction by Maria Flores Letelier, Fernando's daughter, who carefully edited all the pieces and, in her commentary, adds her own interpretations. She took time to say what makes each essay relevant today.

I started my career in the late 1960s as a computer scientist professor and was drawn to Fernando and his work in the mid 1980s because I was encountering management breakdowns in a research institute I was leading. From Fernando's essays I saw like a lightning bolt that my traditional view of information as a collection of facts, and of coordination as exchange of information, completely missed the side of language in which we make commitments, build our identities, and cope with our moods. That was where the management breakdowns were coming from. Once I learned this I was able to lead the organization much more effectively.

Fernando offered another interpretation growing out of this, that education is the learning of practices at increasing levels of skill. This was another lightning bolt that revealed that my approach to teaching was built on the idea that education was transferring information. I developed a manifesto about how engineering education could become vastly better if based on his new principle, and I took it back to the university where I could put it to practice. I developed a design course called "Sense 21" (a new common sense for the 21st century), which became very popular. The students formed an alumni group that continued for ten years after the first time I offered the course. No student of my traditional computing classes wanted to form an alumni group. Fernando's principles were more appealing than many computing principles!

Over the years I became interested in how these principles could help leaders and entrepreneurs be more successful at innovation. This culminated in a book about innovation as a skillful practice for getting others to adopt new ideas into their communities. My second career as a teacher of innovation practices grew of those essays. Now I'm a computer science professor who also teaches innovation

Take this book, settle into a comfortable chair, and let the new insights settle into your system. Soon you will be seeing lightning bolts too.

Peter J. Denning
Distinguished Professor of Computer Science
Co-Author of The Innovator's Way (MIT Press, 2010).

Preface

The essays in this collection are drawn from papers that I wrote with a group of collaborators between 1985 and 2000. During those years, I led the development of enterprises in education (Logonet Inc.), business consulting (Business Design Associates Inc.), and software (Action Technologies, inventor of "coordinator" software). The essays in this collection were prepared for clients and for our own thinking for doing our work. Each essay, with the exception of "Conversations for Action," was initiated with a question I was exploring in our work and challenges with clients. The reflections behind "Conversations for Action" date back to my term in the Allende government in Chile, where the question of communication for getting work done first came to me. I later developed the subject in my dissertation, "Management and Communication in the Office of the Future," at the University of California, Berkeley.

At the core of all of the essays is my understanding of language as the fundamental characteristic of what makes us human. Language has many dimensions. We have words and sounds and writing. But language also has the dimension of acts—the way that we do things with language, and that language does with us. Our rationalistic tradition, in which I was educated originally as an engineer at the Universidad Catolica in Chile, puts its emphasis on facts, the representation of facts, building models, and communicating about the truth of claims. Through life experiences, some of them tougher than others, and profound study of philosophy, I gained the conviction that there is a whole other world that is just as important, and no less rational—a world that is emotional, social, and historical. This is the world in which, in collaboration with others, we bring forth realities, negotiate with each other, and make history happen, all in conversations with each other. It is a world in which language is not merely about notations of facts but also poetical and political invention.

Many of the essays in this collection were constructed in an attempt to bring this other world to people in a way that would empower them to invent a new capacity and facility of readiness to participate in this dimension of our world—to pursue new observations and new skills—and at the same to do that in practical ways, avoiding the hysteria that sometimes pervades philosophical ventures into new worlds of possibility.

I have benefited a lot from the speech act tradition developed by Professor John L. Austin at Oxford, and by Professor John Searle, with whom I did my PhD at the University of California in Berkeley. I have brought what I learned from them and from the tradition to reinterpret the world of business and relationships in a different way—an "ontological" way. Another dimension of language into which I have delved is its hermeneutical dimension: listening and learning to be receptive to our inheritance from traditions are central issues. In my learning, the towering figures in that tradition have been Martin Heidegger and Hans Gadamer. Personally, my chief teacher has been Professor Hubert Dreyfus at the University of California at Berkeley. In the background of all of this, though often not explicitly, has been my interest in our biological being, particularly in the tradition built by Professors Humberto Maturana and Francisco Varela, fellow Chileans and colleagues for many years.

It was during this same period, 1985-2000, that I wrote and published *Understanding Computers and Cognition* with Terry Winograd, *Building Trust In Business, Relationships, and Politics* with Bob Solomon, and *Disclosing New Worlds* with Charles Spinosa and Hubert Dreyfus.

Despite the fact that the papers that follow carry my signature, they all result from collaborations and carry the contributions of many people. The more remarkable contributions to this body of work have been Chauncey Bell, Michael Graves, Charles Spinosa, Alfred ("Bud") Vieira, and my daughter Maria Flores Letelier , with whom I discussed, framed, drafted, and built the papers.

When we started doing this work, computers and networks were just coming along. (I first drafted *Understanding Computers and Cognition* on a Xerox Alto computer, which was one of Steve Jobs' inspirations in designing the early Apple computers.) Providing interpretations and tools for the world that we could see was coming was one of the inspirations and motivations for all of the work since.

Today, the situation is different. The networked and computer-mediated world that I imagined is already here. This world arrives with new political issues—threats to the environment, global warming, the prospect of serious intervention in our biological beings, and so forth—and these demand new thinking. In addition, my obligations in Chile, arising from my term as a senator and as an advisor to the government, have brought me to think about innovation, issues and policy for science and technology, and the tensions brought about by pluralistic and unequal societies. These topics are not addressed in this collection of papers. Something about my thinking on some of these issues can be found in the paper "Entrepreneurship and the wired life: Work in the wake of career," which I wrote in 2000 with John Gray.

I am working with Terry Winograd on the questions of innovation and the new networked world, and I hope to publish something new out of that work. In what we are writing, I hope to bring some of the "old," sampled here, along with new foundations for thinking and acting in the world at which we have arrived today, in particular for university and business audiences.

One of my most recent collaborative projects is one that I have had the pleasure to work on with my daughters Gloria and Javiera: developing skills and sensibilities for living in pluralistic networks. As I mentioned above, we now live in a global, highly connected world, yet we don't yet know how to live together in what we call "pluralistic networks," networks in which people of different backgrounds, nationalities, cultures, and belief systems commit to living together, respecting their differences, and collaborating to create value for each other. There are many obstacles to pluralistic networks, including social barriers, political barriers, and our own emotional backgrounds, which show up as feelings, attitudes, or prejudices. If we are unable to navigate these obstacles, we are left with a significantly weakened capacity to collaborate, to innovate, and to coordinate efficiently and effectively.

The good news is that the work that we have been doing shows that by learning new skills and sensibilities, we can learn to live and work in pluralistic networks. We have invested significant time and effort developing and delivering educational programs designed to build these kinds of skills and sensibilities. We are convinced that the traditional educational model of acquiring knowledge and applying new information does not work for this purpose. Our focus has been to create new contexts for the development of what are often referred to as the soft skills: the ability to coordinate our commitments, ability to cultivate trust, ability to listen, ability to manage moods, etc. By combining the work that we have been doing with many of our corporate clients for the last twenty years, with spaces for ontological reflection and new technologies around immersive game play, we have been developing these contexts and enabling people to develop their abilities to work with others, despite their differences, with respect and with trust. I look forward to continuing to develop this work, and I invite you to join us in exploring, building, and playing in these spaces with us at Pluralistic Networks, Inc.

Until now, although these papers are as relevant today as when they were written, I have been reluctant to publish them, as they were written in a different context and time with a particular audience in mind. However, my daughters have convinced me that these papers are not only relevant, but that they would be useful to people in their current form without any need to update them. The existence of this collection of papers results almost entirely from my daughter Maria's discipline as a philosopher and from her love for her father. The selection of this set of papers and the editorial preparation for publication are entirely hers.

Fernando Flores
Berkeley, CA April 2012

Acknowledgements

I would like to acknowledge all the clients, colleagues, BDA and Logonet employees, and academic allies who participated in the ongoing dialogue that kept the work of alive all of these years. To name everyone would require writing an anthology. I am sure that most of you know who you are. Alfred ("Bud") Vieira, Bob Dunham, and Michael Graves, in particular, acted as key contributors, at different moments in history, to several of the works in this collection of essays. Long-term practioners and collaborators who put this work to practice with organizations include Mario Valdivia, Christopher Davis, Guillermo Wechsler, Peter Luzmore, and Billy Glennon's consultancy VISION Consulting.

I have had the honor of working with my family members in all three of the enterprises I founded. My daughters Gloria, Maria, and Javiera each played important roles at BDA. My sons Rodrigo and Pablo played key roles in the software company Action Technologies, where the conversations for action framework was developed into software. My son-in-laws Bill Fine and Rodolfo Larrea also played key roles at BDA. And my wife Gloria was a founding member of Logonet and later became a leading executive coach at BDA. Working with family members is challenging for everyone involved, and this can only be accomplished if the family believes in the work and finds it meaningful. Each of these individuals accepted my invitation because they sincerely believed the experience would allow them to make a bigger impact in the future. My family's strong beliefs in all that I was developing inspired me even further. For this, I am thankful to all of them.

I would like to thank Steve Canny, who helped us overcome some technical challenges in converting the files from an older technology to a current one.

To footnote John Searle in this collection would be insufficient. John Searle's *Speech Acts: An Essay in the Philosophy of Language* (Cambridge University Press, 1969) and J. L. Austin's *How to Do Things with Words* (second edition, Oxford

University Press, 1975) were the works that inspired me while sitting in a Chilean jail for three-and-a-half years under the Pinochet regime.

Hubert Dreyfus is another great influence. His many works, including *the Dreyfus Model of Skill Acquisition,* about how students acquire skills both through formal training and practice, and his exposition of Martin Heidegger's *Being in Time Being-in-the-world: A Commentary on Heidegger's Being and Time, Division I* (Cambridge, MA: MIT Press, 1991) greatly influenced my thinking on listening and attunement to the background cultural style in which we operate. Moreover, the Saturday morning breakfasts at Fat Apples with Bert over the last thirty years provided much food for thought as well.

Finally, I wish to give a special acknowledgement to Chauncey Bell, who worked closer than anyone to me in the start-up and management of two of the businesses where much of the thought leadership in these papers was developed (BDA and Action Technologies). The ongoing dialogue and invention process between Chauncey and myself gave birth to what would become the "loop", the "action workflow", and "commitment-based management". Chauncey has been and continues to be among my closest collaborators.

Introduction

By Maria Flores Letelier

Instilling a Culture of Commitment in Our Working Relationships

While the essays in this book were written sixteen to twenty years ago, I see them as more relevant today than ever. That is why I was determined, in the midst of two pregnancies and caring for newly born babies, to find a way to dig up some of the most relevant essays that my father wrote then and make them publicly available for the first time. As I re-read these essays many years later, at first I was a bit taken aback by the awkwardness of some of the writing—the grandeur of the words, the fierceness of many of the claims, and the obvious nature of many of the questions posed. Then it became clear to me that because the thinking was so new at the time, my father had to develop a whole new language to make these points. The idea that we invent reality together in the commitments we make to each other when we speak went against not only current academic thinking then about human behavior, but also our commonsense understanding of that topic at the time. He was not writing for the self-help category of books, a category that did not exist at the time. He was bringing a human dimension to the world of work, organizations, and business.

Today, it is clear to me that much of what my father was anticipating, even as far back as when he was a prisoner of the Pinochet regime in Chile, was the importance of instilling a culture of commitment in what would become a dominantly capitalistic world. His thinking goes to the heart of not only how people transact and negotiate in a capitalistic world, but also how, in coordinating, there is much more than self interest at stake. Indeed, we are making commitments to each other, and that entails caring for the concerns of each party. If we only make explicit the self-interested dimension, then we will design organizations, and ultimately our social values, accordingly. Fernando Flores made a brave move forward, proposing that we design our organizations around the networks of commitments being made and that these commitments be made explicit.

The academic thinking behind the networks of commitments framework is the theory of speech acts that describes "networks of directives and commissives," the theory Fernando Flores build upon. Directives, such as requests and offers, are spoken acts that attempt to get the person being spoken to, to perform some action. Commissives are spoken acts in which the person being spoken to commits to some future course of action. He argues that certain speech acts, particularly requests, promises, offers, assessments, and declarations, serve as building blocks for activating and fulfilling commitments in working relationships and, hence, in organizations.

The essays in this book are all about how to effectively make commitments that allow us to create something of value, to generate value for ourselves and for others in the world. In essence, they are about instilling a culture of commitment in our work with others, whether that be in an organization, our own start-up, or even in working together as a family to get ahead or raise children. He was anticipating what would become the greatest challenge of capitalism hence far: unregulated free markets that coexist with value creation for the world at large.

With the recent collapse of our financial system and some of the major corporations that exemplified the best of capitalism, it's becoming clearer to many academics and business leaders that something more is needed. Whether we call it a new form of capitalism or a "kinder capitalism," as Bill Gates has described it, the point is that people work together to produce value, not just for self-interest. The networks of commitments/conversations for action framework for designing organizations makes explicit who is creating value and for whom value is being created, and what are the promises being completed that act as value producers at every step of the way.

The notion of "social responsibility" is taking on a new dimension. Corporations are starting to recognize that social responsibility cannot exist as an afterthought. It cannot be an isolated public relations or charitable contributions organization. The core business has to think about how its products, manufacturing processes, business processes, employee relations, services, and role in the community impact the world. Designing work to produce value is very different from designing work for maximizing the self-interest of each party involved. I have had the privilege of working with organizations in designing and launching offerings that improve the quality of life for those in lower income communities. Time and time again, I learned that solely focusing on the design of the product or service itself is insufficient; each role in the business process had to be designed with the key value producing promises that would impact the final offering. Personal agendas are replaced with a missionary type responsibility for customers and for the organizations. As I re-read the essays in this collection, it became clearer that the seeds for this design are here, and that is why so many people have requested these essays over the last twenty years. And that is why I found myself employing the framework in my work as well.

Today, many of the former consultants, coaches, students, and clients that practice the methodologies described here discuss this phenomenon as "working relationships" —what makes some effective and others not so. By combining the disciplines of philosophy, linguistics, computer science, and management, Fernando Flores developed a unique theory of work and organizations that has had numerous practical applications. The seeds of these classic works were first developed in his dissertation, "Management and the Office of the Future," which was written in 1980.

"The process of communication should be designed to bring with it a major awareness about the occurrence of commitments. Every member's knowledge about his participation in the network of commitment must be reinforced and developed."

(Management and Communication In The Office Of The Future p.70).

In working relationships, each member has a role in making something happen. Each member is accountable for a promise in the commitment network or chain. Today, these tools are starting to enter organizations as they try to make explicit the roles and responsibilities of various functions in the organizations. Those functions are performed by people—human beings—, each with distinct talents and dispositions for taking on various roles. As people changes occur, roles maybe redefined, yet the central promises of the role remain explicit. If a particular individual will not fulfill these, it becomes clear that the value producing promises must be fulfilled by some role in the organization; failure to fulfill those promises will impact negatively the value produced by the organization.

Still, the historical tendency is to describe titles and activities, not promises. Accountabilities get lost as organizational changes are made. In making "promises" explicit, it becomes clear that each person in the commitment net-work is accountable to other people, as promises are to someone else. In other words, the human dimension of working relationships becomes the focus in designing work and organizations.

The human dimension is also brought forth to the center in my father's theory of communication. He challenges the assertion that when people com-municate, we simply pass information back and forth. Instead, he proposes that people get things done—share interpretations and make commitments to each other that take care of their concerns—thereby shifting their future expecta-tions, possibilities, and, in turn, the direction of their future. In addition to promises, requests, and declarations, which play a central role in "conversations for action," he adds yet a more complex layer of human interaction with assess-ments and assertions. People evaluate and are evaluated by others, probably the trickiest part of working relationships, in the form of assessments and asser-tions. And these take place against a background of "moods."

My father sometimes tells the story of how the importance of making assess-ments and grounding these on assertions came to him as he reflected about what happened with the fall of President Allende's government. He recalls speaking with the president to convey his assessment of Pinochet and report rumors that he heard of a secret coup d'etat that was being planned. He describes a feeling of paralysis that came over him as he stood in front of the president searching for the best way to frame the assessment. Assessments, as he now describes, are tied up with moods; it is insufficient to just make a grounded assessment, one must speak to the mood that a person is in. He now sees that the appropriate mood was not there at the time. Organizations can instill particular moods, such as the moods of wonder, ambition, resoluteness, serenity, and conviction, that allow people to make the appropriate assessments at the right time. Preparing back-ground moods lays the groundwork for coordination and invention in organiza-tions and working together. He claims that language owns us; it speaks through us in who we are as cultural, historical beings.

The networks of commitments/conversations for action thought leadership has been cited in more than three thousand books. Fernando Flores is recog-nized as a leader in the world of business process design, computers, cogni-tion, and education. *Understanding Computers and Cognition: A New Foundation for Design*, with Dr. Terry Winograd, was named the Best Information Science book of 1987 by the American Society for Information Science, and recognized by *Byte* magazine as one of the all-time twenty most influential books on information technology. His work laid the foundation for much of the current understanding about action workflow and commitment management theory.

For many years, this work was available only in private papers. In this book, I have selected and edited a group of essays and placed them in an effective order for the reader. I made an attempt to leave the essays as close to their original form as possible. I edited with an editor's eye, deleting repetitiveness and elaborating on points that seemed to be central. I often changed a title and reorganized an essay around a central theme, since these were often written assuming the audience already understood the background theme.

Some of the essays are in the public domain, while others remained private. I have included both. When I observed redundancies, I tried to bring out what I perceived as the central claim in each and included more than one version. This is especially the case for the first section of the book, where I included different versions of "Conversations for Action," with a distinct emphasis that I brought to the center in each essay.

I begin with, and give most importance to, the classic essay entitled "Conversations for Action," as this essay has influenced thousands since it was first written in the early '90s. Many consider the essay to be "classic," as it provides simple and effective distinctions for observing how we invent what we do together in conversations through certain basic speech acts. Indeed if one Googles "Conversations for Action" and "Commitment Based Management," there are endless pages that come up with practitioners utilizing this framework in their work, many of them former students. Some are utilizing the work for organizational change, some for life coaching, and others for business process design. These former students and practioners provided inspiration for putting this collection together in one place.

Then there are a few essays that elaborate further on practical applications of the conversations for action framework. The first section ends with another classic, "Assessments and Assertions," an essay that has allowed many to have more effective conversations regarding their observations of each other and the work being produced.

The first essays elaborate more on all that is entailed in making effective assessments of others. The second section of the book introduces a series of essays that I believe are about building commitment. They are about the connection between language, moods, and building trust.

The final section introduces the other side of my father's works: all that is entailed in listening and being attuned to what is in the cultural background.

While the title of this collection refers to Fernando Flores' classic structure of conversations for action, I thought it was important to introduce a few distinctions which went on to form much of his later thinking regarding how "language owns us as historical, cultural beings." Some of this thinking is elaborated in *Disclosing New Worlds, Entrepreneurship, Democratic Action, and the Cultivation of Solidarity* and some is part of ongoing development. As the structure proposed by "Conversations for Action" became implemented in organizations and people's lives, it became clear that conversations take place against a historical context. When people engage in conversation and invent the future, we must cultivate skills for listening and tuning in to concerns of others and to the background cultural style that influences both parties. The essays on concerns and listening are written in a more theoretical style, as these were written for an internal audience, i.e., for consultant training development. Still, it seemed important to introduce some of these distinctions to further enrich the "conversations for actions" and networks of commitments structure to get the full view of what my father began proposing many years back.

While the book is meant to be a collection of essays rather than one coherent book, the essays all share the same view of language as "expressive" rather than "instrumental," or conveying information. When people engage in conversations, commitments are made, and spaces of possibilities are opened up. Therefore, the theme is of "instilling a culture of commitment" in our working relationships. In a different way, each essay is implicitly addressing the challenge of our working relationships and distinctions for instilling a culture of commitment through language, building the right moods and trust, and listening.

Today, people are increasingly stressed by their working relationships. We hear stories of people coming home wanting to simply disconnect, to shut out all the stressful working relationships they must deal with on a daily basis. With our networked technology, e-mail, smartphones, chat, and so forth, disconnecting is becoming increasingly more difficult. If we do not respond right away to an e-mail, for instance, we stress out about appearing irresponsible. We are caught in the game of trying to balance endless individual interests; "If I let him have this win, maybe I will get this next win" type thinking. I hope that this group of essays plants the seeds for another way of thinking about our working relationships, one that instills a commitment culture, allowing us to think about what we are creating of value together rather than the ongoing stress of attempting to calculate tradeoffs of individual interests.

PART 1

The Basic Elements

CHAPTER 1

Conversations For Action

Imagine this scene: You're taking part in a regular staff meeting. Several staff members complain that during the previous two weeks, work orders were filled out sloppily, which caused delays in providing services to some customers. You spend ten minutes discussing the issue and what might be done about it, and the meeting is adjourned. Nobody was charged with taking care of the problem, and staff members leave with a slightly unsettled feeling. A week later, the same issue is brought up in the staff meeting, and the situation from last time is replayed.

We're all familiar with similar situations in our work, situations where we don't work effectively together, situations where the present seems to keep repeating itself and it doesn't feel as if we're moving forward. It's not clear who will address what, so people begin to blame one another. Then we find ourselves focused on pointing fingers rather than on producing value for the business and for customers.

Breakdowns in communication between people have always been a frequent issue in the workplace as well as in life. Whether you're a company trying to ensure that your teams, departments, and business units are working with and not against each other, or you're an entrepreneur or self-employed contractor who often feels that his or her needs aren't understood, breakdowns in coordination and communication impede effective work from happening. Worse, people begin to feel as if their work is meaningless, that they're not producing value for others or receiving value from doing the work for themselves.

In this chapter, we'll look at how we create our work, where we produce breakdowns, and how we make action happen. *We propose that we make things happen in the commitments we make to each other, and that we make these commitments in conversations.* To understand how we do this, we must first challenge our common understanding of communication.

Our Common Understanding

We typically think of "communication" as conveying to each other our desires and intentions for the future, and "action" as getting our bodies in motion to accomplish those goals. After all, having conversations is what we do when we're "just thinking about" action, before we "just do it."

Our everyday understanding of action and language is strongly influenced by two broad assumptions about how people coordinate with each other to get things done. The first assumption is that people have clear needs and desires, and human language gives us the ability to transfer information about our desires from one person to another. The second assumption is that action consists of the physical movements necessary to satisfy those desires. Together, these assumptions support the interpretation that in conversation, we share information about what we want to have happen in the future, and in action, we use our bodies to carry out those intentions.

This may be an adequate framework for understanding our simplest needs, wants, and most routine transactions. When you buy a soda at a hot dog stand, or a surgeon asks for a scalpel in the operating room, the future is clear and immediate. Language can masquerade as mere transmission of information here, because both the desire and the action that will satisfy it are so narrowly specified. The situation is different, though, when you're inventing a new product or closing a deal with a client. Your customer may not know exactly what will ideally satisfy him or her. No amount of information will allow you to predict exactly how his or her needs will change in the future. In these situations, you don't need to predict and manage mere movement, but rather *invent and manage a set of ongoing conversations for producing satisfaction for your customers.*

People often—perhaps even usually—don't have clear, specified desires, and language isn't the transfer of information from one mind to another. People don't merely use language to communicate their desires about the future; they

4

create the future in language together by making commitments to each other. Conversation, then, is not merely a prelude to action, *it is its very essence.*

This view has two principal advantages over our more common understanding of language and action. First, it presents us with the possibility of an elegantly simple way to observe and manage how people coordinate their actions. We'll demonstrate that while people's needs and intentions are represented in a nearly infinite variety, we can distinguish an inevitable structure for the coordination of action in language that's composed of only a few basic elements. Secondly, viewing action as coordination in language greatly expands our ability to deal with the future flexibly and creatively. When action is viewed as physical movement, the future must be predicted and planned in advance. Understanding that we create the future in language gives us more room to maneuver and respond to unexpected changes.

The Basic Structure of a Conversation for Action

This perspective—managing conversations rather than information—of human action may seem counterintuitive, but it can dramatically simplify our understanding of action and work. While we can generate an infinite amount of information about people's desires, we can distinguish just one simple conversational structure—the conversation for action—in which people coordinate their actions. Furthermore, this structure consists of variations on just a few basic moves in language, or what's referred to as "speech acts." In making a speech act, you're not simply conveying information. You're making a commitment about how you and your listeners will coordinate your actions in the future.

In its simplest form, the conversation for action consists of four separate speech acts:

1. Request or offer,
2. Promise or acceptance,
3. Declaration of completion, and
4. Declaration of satisfaction.

We can observe these distinctions in our own and in other people's speech. The first two moves involve the exchange of a request and a promise. In making a request, you're indicating your desire to have something happen in the future. When someone accepts your request and promises to fulfill it, he or she commits himself or herself to making sure that what you asked for eventually actually happens in a way that satisfies you. After the exchange, you have a common orientation toward fulfilling the request that influences how each of you will act in the future.

Let's look at these speech acts more closely so you can start observing them and build new practices with them, which will enable you to become more effective in your daily work.

Request and Offer

There are two ways of initiating a conversation for action: making a request or an offer.

Making a request of someone sounds like:

"Please meet me at the office half an hour earlier tomorrow morning so that we can get a head start on the performance assessments."

"I ask that the staff meet once a week from now on."

"I'm not pleased with the new connection XYZ Electricity Company built for me the other day, and I insist that you send out a service man to take care of it."

"Everybody is to follow the safety regulations."

"Pass me the stapler, please"

In speaking, a request can show up in many variations, such as "I ask," "insist," "order," "plead," "beg," or "Stand up," "Help!" "Out!" and so forth. The different tones indicate the relationship we have with each other; the various verbs and expressions belong to the basic distinction of "request."

When others agree to our requests, we're changing the future. Let's look at an example between two different areas of business. When a customer calls an area business unit (ABU) to request electrical service and the customer service representative (CSR) takes the call, she might ask some questions about the customer's specific needs. They agree on a certain date for the installation of the new service to take place, and the CSR promises the customer that the service men will be out at the mutually agreed-upon time. In this brief conversation, they're building their future together: the CSR, as a representative for the ABU, made a commitment to provide the electrical service, and the customer made a commitment by accepting the conditions for the delivery of the service. Based on these commitments, the customer as well as the CSR will take certain actions in order to fulfill his/her commitments. The customer will clear his schedule so he'll be present when the service men arrive to build the service; or he might ask his wife to be available when the service men arrive at their house. The CSR fills out a work order, speaks to the service men about the job, makes sure they're available and know about the customer's specific needs, etc.

Fundamental Elements of a Request

The act of requesting requires that all the following elements appear in the listening of the relevant parties:

1. Speaker (specific identity)
2. Hearer (specific identity)
3. Conditions of satisfaction (COS) stated in accordance with the standard practices of a community
4. Background of obviousness sufficient to the request
5. Specified time for fulfillment of the request:

   Spoken   COS due

   $Time_1$ $Time_2$
6. Future action to be performed by the hearer
7. Brings forth something missing: a new possibility
8. Presupposition of hearer's ability to fulfill
9. Sincerity
10. The speaker and hearer share concerns that make the conditions of satisfaction relevant

Offers

People don't just respond to requests. We also try to address the concerns of others through offers. Businesses attempt to anticipate their customers' concerns and design conditions of satisfaction that customers will be interested in purchasing. In this respect, an offer can be interpreted as a conditional promise: a company promises that it will produce some conditions of satisfaction for a customer, given that it receives money in exchange. A conversation for action that starts with an offer in this way has its own slightly different structure. In this case, the first phase is the offer, a conditional promise.

Examples of how to initiate offers include:

"Here's a user guide for you. It'll help you to learn about the new software program."

"We offer you a power efficiency audit of your entire school building, which could cut your electric bill by 20 percent."

"I offer to cover the office for you this afternoon. Would you like me to?"

"Would it help you if we talked about the upset you had with the customer?"

As you can see, an offer also shows up in many variations in our speech. However, the various forms of expression, as indicated in the examples above, belong to the basic distinction of "offer."

We only can produce action together if we have a mutual commitment from both the customer and the performer. In the case of a request, the customer makes the request and the performer either promises to fulfill the request, declines, or negotiates with the customer until they reach a mutual agreement. In the case of an offer, the performer makes an offer and the customer either accepts the offer, declines, or negotiates with the performer until they reach a mutual agreement.

For example, suppose that a regional sales manager is attending a meeting and asks one of his salespeople to prepare a report for him on the status of her trading area. If the salesperson promises to fulfill this request, she must now plan to allot time and resources to preparing the report. This may involve changes in her schedule, including when and whether she completes other previously planned projects. Likewise, the manager will continue in his work as if the report can be taken for granted; he won't ask another person also to prepare the same report, or work on it himself. Although we usually only think of promises as involving commitments, notice that the future that's built in this exchange is mutual. The manager may be angry if the report isn't completed in time for his meeting, but the salesperson may also be annoyed if she spends two days preparing a report that's filed away and never used. Both unfulfilled promises and unnecessary requests can destroy trust between people.

Here's an example in the case of a request: Suppose I say to you, as in one of the above examples, "Please meet me at the office half an hour earlier tomorrow morning so we can get a head start on the performance assessments." In this case, I'm in the role of the customer, requesting that you do something for me. Let's assume you promise to be there, which then makes you the performer.

Here's an example in the case of an offer: Suppose I say to you: "I offer to cover the office for you this afternoon." In this case, I'm in the role of the performer, offering to do something for you. You accept my offer, which then makes you the customer.

Breakdowns are easily produced when we don't listen carefully to whether a promise was made or not, or if we're not clear about who holds which role. Let's go back to the above example, where I made the request of you "to meet me at the office half an hour earlier tomorrow morning...." Suppose that instead of making the request explicitly of you, I'd make the request in a general way to the whole office staff. The next morning only three of six staff members arrive half an hour earlier, and I get furious about the other three staff members' unreliability. In fact, though, what had happened had nothing to do with their reliability. As the customer, I'd simply not noticed that they hadn't promised to be there in the morning; consequently, some of them didn't see themselves as performers and didn't show up. (See "Fundamental Elements of a Request or Promise— Including Offer.")

In the above examples, you can see how "we make something happen" or "produce action in speech" by making requests, offers, and promises. To illustrate this point further, let's look at one more example: Imagine your office for a moment; at some moment in time, someone in the Smith Electricity Company saw the need for further office space and requested that the facility department acquire the appropriate space. The facility department promised to have the required space by a certain time. Once the space was found, it had to be furnished, so the facility department put out a request for bids from office furniture stores. The store with the best bid got the deal and provided the furniture. Once the office was furnished, a representative from Information Systems (IS) visited your office to present the newest developments in computer technology, and together the office staff decided to go with one of the IS offers. A few weeks later, a new terminal arrived on your desk.

Fundamental Elements of an Offer/Promise

The acts of offering and promising require that all the following elements appear in the listening of the relevant parties:

1. Speaker (specific identity)
2. Hearer (specific identity)
3. Conditions of satisfaction (COS) stated in accordance with the standard practices of a community
4. Background of obviousness sufficient to the offer/promise
5. Specified time for fulfillment of the offer/promise:

Spoken	COS due
$Time_1$	$Time_2$

6. Future action to be performed by the speaker
7. Brings forth something missing: a new possibility
8. Presupposition of speaker's ability to fulfill
9. Sincerity
10. The speaker and hearer share concerns that make the conditions of satisfaction relevant

Counteroffer

Although we typically don't like to do either, declining and revoking requests are important moves in coordinating action with others. When you fail to decline a request that you're unable to fulfill, the other person may be counting on you and running out of time to look for an alternative. Another possibility in this kind of situation is the counteroffer. In a counteroffer, you decline to fulfill the person's original request, but promise to complete other conditions that address his or her concerns. You may also commit to commit; that is, notify the person making the request that you're unable to say one way or the other now, but you promise to give him or her a commitment at a later, specified time. Finally, at any point in the conversation, the person making the request can cancel, letting the promisor know that his or her assistance is no longer needed, thus avoiding useless work.

Conditions of Satisfaction

It's also important to note here that in our interpretation, a person doesn't make a request simply to obtain a thing—that is, a concrete object or an event. People make requests because they have concerns for the future in their dealings with others. In the example a few pages ago, the manager had some concern in the meeting that prompted him to request a report; perhaps he needed it to support a request for more funding. If the report is the best he's ever seen, but arrives too late for the meeting, it's useless. Accordingly, we say that in making requests and promises, we aren't specifying particular objects or events to be produced, but agreeing on conditions of satisfaction that will address the concerns we have in the world.

When making a request or an offer, we have conditions we like to be fulfilled by the performer. These conditions might be explicit or implicit. Let's use the example "Pass me the stapler, please" to illustrate what we mean by this:

Situation I: I turn to my administrative assistant at the next desk over and ask for him to pass me the stapler. He passes me the stapler, I say thank you and start stapling a bunch of documents. I'm pleased and keep doing my work.

Situation II: I ask my administrative assistant to pass me the stapler. He passes me the stapler, I say thank you, and when I start to staple my documents, the stapler doesn't work. In a slightly irritated tone, I say: "This damn thing is out of staples; what good does it do for me?" This time I'm obviously not pleased, since I couldn't get my work done.

In making my request, I was interested in getting a working stapler so I could take care of my documents before they spread out all over the place. I had a particular concern I needed to take care of, and in order to do so, I needed the stapler to operate properly. Otherwise, it's of no use to me. In Situation II, you can see that my administrative assistant delivered on his promise to pass the stapler, but he didn't fulfill my conditions of satisfaction. Therefore, we say that in making requests, offers, and promises, we don't specify particular objects or events to be produced, but rather agree on conditions of satisfaction that will address the concerns we have.

Declaration of Completion and Declaration of Satisfaction

Declarations of Completion: After the conditions of satisfaction have been requested, there's a period of time in which the promisor is engaged in their production. In other words, once the conditions of satisfaction are clear and a request or offer is accepted, the performer can get to work.

At some point in this process, he resolves that he's fulfilled the conditions, and he tells the requestor that he's done. We say that this notice of completion is a kind of declaration. A declaration is a speech act in which we create new possibilities for action just by the act of speaking. The most obvious examples of this phenomenon involve the use of institutional authority; for example, the CEO of a company may declare that someone will be the new vice president of marketing. From then on, the new vice president, as well as other people in and outside of the organization, will act in accordance with that declaration.

Similarly, in a conversation for action, the promisor's declaration of completion changes the actions that are now possible for the requestor. For instance, the salesperson in our earlier example may call her manager to let him know that the report he requested is ready. That declaration of completion changes his world from one in which he's expecting a sales report to one in which he's prepared to take action in his meeting. This isn't the last move in the conversation. Finally, after looking over the report, the manager indicates that he's satisfied, perhaps by simply saying "thank you." This is also a declaration in which the requestor lets the promisor know that his concerns have indeed been addressed by what the promisor has produced. This final declaration closes the conversation for both parties.

In one of the examples above, I requested my staff to meet me at the office half an hour earlier the next morning so we could get a head start on the performance assessments. Let's say all the staff members promised to be there the next morning. In order to do so, some of them had to rearrange things at home, such as getting the kids to school earlier than usual or asking the babysitter to arrive half an hour earlier or making sure that their spouse would step in and take over some of these chores. Then, some might've had to catch an earlier bus or take their own car to work instead of joining the car pool at the usual time. All of them had to do something in order to fulfill my request. When they arrived the next morning at 7 a.m., they were ready to meet with me. By arriving at the agreed-upon time, they declared that they'd completed what I'd asked them to do. In turn, I was happy that we could get started early with the day and get our performance assessments done. I said, "Thank you for coming in early," by which I declared that I was satisfied with what they'd done for me.

Now the whole conversation has come to a completion. Be mindful that the conversation isn't done when the performer declares the work complete. *The customer has the final say on whether the conversation has ended.* Suppose all of my staff came ten to fifteen minutes late to the early morning meeting. The conversation would have taken a different turn. As the customer, I would've been quite dissatisfied and would have demanded of them to come in half an hour earlier again the following morning, until they all did so. Finally, I would've declared satisfaction and the conversation would be complete.

The basic request and offer loops outlined above constitute complete conversations for action in their simplest form. Often, though, such conversations are more complicated and may include a number of variations of the four basic moves. For instance, if you're unable to fulfill another person's request, you may decline to do so. Seen as a speech act, a decline is a kind of promise; you're saying that you do not want to provide the requested conditions of satisfaction. Similarly, if you've already promised but find yourself unable to fulfill, you may revoke your prior commitment.

One very important class of declarations is social in character—you declare a conversation complete, or a commitment fulfilled, by saying, "Thank you." You declare, thereby, your social acknowledgment that the commitment is fulfilled.

Conversely, in cases where a commitment is broken, you may declare responsibility in the matter by saying, "I apologize."

Fundamental Elements of a Declaration

The act of declaring requires that all the following elements appear in the listening of the relevant parties:

1. Speaker (specific identity)
2. Hearer(s) (a community)
3. Brings forth a new distinction (examples: a new entity, a new identity, a new practice, a new possibility)
4. In an existing background of obviousness

5. A community (the hearers) grants power to the speaker to author the declaration
6. The community is committed to maintain the declaration over time
7. The declaration is manifested in our actions of living together
8. Sincerity

Conclusion

When you speak and listen in conversations for action, you make commitments. (Later, we'll also discuss conversations for possibilities.) That's all you do. You request, offer, promise, assess, assert, counteroffer, or declare. You may make an assertion: "The report is on your desk." In making an assertion, you've already committed yourself to providing evidence in support of your assertion. In other words, people sometimes ask, "Where on my desk? I did not see it there."

You may then make a declaration such as, "The report was badly done." Judgments are one kind of declaration. Other declarations produce new possibilities. For example:

"We could begin to report by electronic mail." Or "We're now open for business" (i.e., new institutions or situations). You may even declare new objects and things: an inventor declares the invention of a new device.

Requests are made in this way: you request that someone perform an action for you at some time in the future. To do so, you must formally specify the time you request the action: "Bring me the report on Wednesday the eighth, before noon."

This request may be heard as, "I request that you bring me the...." Furthermore, everyone involved must understand the conditions required to satisfy the request. In other words, both of you presumably know which report the speaker's talking about.

You may promise to perform an action at some time in the future, perhaps in response to a request from someone. Or perhaps you make a promise in response to a proposal or offer, where your promise depends on the other person's accepting your conditions of satisfaction. For example:

"I promise to bring you the report before noon, Wednesday, the eighth."

"I offer to bring you the report at noon on Tuesday, the seventh, if you'll approve my working at home on it on Monday."

As with a request, you must specify time, and the conditions of satisfaction must be mutually clear.

Finally, for effective action to take place, you must at some point declare the action complete. Often people fulfill promises but forget to communicate to the concerned party the fulfillment, and then they complain because the concerned party does not acknowledge completion. Both acts are crucial for effective action to continue occurring.

We've made some claims that go against our common understanding of the role that language plays in the coordination of action. We've argued that language isn't something we use to talk about action; it's how we create our common future. People don't have conversations for action to specify some object that must be produced or procedure that must be followed. They have them to keep themselves oriented toward a common future that they're all committed to. The unfolding of this future can be observed in one simple structure of a few basic speech acts, which is the equivalent of the periodic table of the elements for cooperative action. Anywhere that people are coordinating their actions, in whatever language, you'll find that they're doing so by making offers and requests, making and fulfilling promises, and declaring satisfaction.

Speech Acts Review Part 1

Speech Act	Action	Required Elements	Examples	What is produced
Declare	A speaker declares a new world of possibilities for action in a community.	-Person making the declaration has the authority to make the declaration.	"We are founding a new company called ABC that will provide...to customers." "We are going to lay off 10 percent of the staff." "We're going to do a new release."	Leadership and a new context for action for taking care of the concerns of the community that listens to the declaration and makes it effective.

Request	A speaker asks a listener, a potential performer, to take care of something that the speaker is concerned about.	-Conditions of satisfaction. -Background of obviousness. - Specified time for fulfillment of the request.	"Can you get me a flight to Boston in time for my meeting?" An application for a mortgage conveys a request.	-Expectation on part of speaker that concern will be addressed -Commitment to action on the part of listener.
Promise	A speaker or "performer" promises to care of something that a listener or "customer" is concerned about.	-Same as request	"I am responsible for increasing sales by 10% this next quarter" "You can count on me to pick up the children at 2:00 tomorrow from school"	-Expectation on part of listener that concern will be addressed -Commitment to action on the part of speaker.
Offer	A speaker or "performer" offers or conditionally promises to take care of something that they perceive the listener or "client" care about.	-Same as request	"Can I offer you dinner" "I offer X for your company" "I will develop a new set of products for this company"	-An interest on the part of the listener to what is being offered. -Confidence on the part of the listener that the speaker is capable of producing what is being offered. -Commitment to a new future and to action on the part of both parties.

CHAPTER 2

Effective Coordination Through Conversations For Action

E ffective coordination is essential for any company's success. Poor coordination jeopardizes important business commitments both inside and outside the enterprise. It's a form of friction, a kind of "sand in the gears" that produces delays, distrust, and waste throughout the enterprise. In today's environment, when responsiveness to customers and the market is critical, companies can no longer afford to tolerate this waste. Savvy business executives look for ways to improve coordination to ensure that people, teams, and entire departments are in synch, working together to produce value for customers and shareholders.

To date, the most substantial work on coordinating people and processes has evolved from industrial engineering and information technology traditions. This work concentrated on improving material, paper, and data flows and on giving people quicker access to information. Designers have made great advances in organizing work and in getting material and information to the right people at the right time. But there are issues of coordination more fundamental that haven't benefited from the same rigorous treatment until recently. These issues are about coordinating people rather than things or information flows, and

17

about building coherence between people's interpretations, intentions, commitments, and relationships. This is the historically thorny "soft" side of management, involving questions like:

Why are we performing these tasks and activities in the first place?

How do we distinguish work that creates value for the customer from work that's simply bureaucratic waste?

How do we stress teamwork and give people more autonomy, yet still be clear on who's accountable for what?

How do we ensure that everyone has the same understanding of the context and purpose of the work and their role in it, so that people act in unison?

How do we build stronger, trusting relationships internally as well as with customers?

Even in companies that have reengineered material flows and information processes, there's a form of miscoordination and waste that remains widespread. We'll detail some of the fundamental distinctions of a discipline to uncover this waste, and describe how to design effectively in these areas of management.

The Cycle of Miscoordination and Distrust: An Example

Consider this short story: On Monday morning, one of the company's executives asks a sales manager for a meeting to discuss the progress of a recently initiated marketing project, which is directed at making the sales team more customer-oriented. They schedule a meeting for 10 a.m. on Wednesday. To prepare for that meeting, the manager decides that he needs an update on the project's development. That morning, he asks three senior marketing representatives, John, Sue, and Kirk, for a report that includes assessments on the performance of the entire sales team, statistics on the number of new customers generated, and a list of recurrent customer complaints. He tells them he needs the report by the end of the day on Tuesday, but doesn't tell them why he needs it. The three sales reps agree to do the report.

Pressed with other responsibilities, each of the senior sales reps puts off working on the report until the next day. On Tuesday, however, each is as busy as the day before. John prepares his assessment on the sales team's performance but doesn't bother with the statistics on new customers or the list of current customer complaints; Sue and Kirk, he thinks, are more familiar with those areas anyway. In the meantime, Sue and Kirk each prepares his or her assessment on

18

performance and draws up a list of customer complaints, but neither prepares statistical information. At the end of the day when the three come together to exchange reports, they realize that no one prepared the statistical information their manager specifically requested. They decide to tell him that they'll have it first thing Wednesday morning.

Once in the manager's office, though, the manager explains to them that the statistical information will be useless to him if he doesn't have it until the morning, because he won't have time to look it over before the meeting with his boss, and this was the reason he'd asked for it in the first place. Further, after briefly skimming the reports, the manager notices that the assessments aren't consistent; in fact, in some instances, they're contradictory. With some disappointment and more than a little frustration, he tells the reps that what they've submitted does nothing to help him prepare for tomorrow's meeting. Frantically, he calls the executive to postpone the meeting, but he's already left for the day. He turns to the three sales reps and asks them to stay late to help him prepare for the meeting. Even though each had previous plans for the evening, they agree. After making a few phone calls to cancel their engagements, the four spend the next several hours preparing the manager for the next day's meeting.

We could cite several reasons that lead to that unfortunate conclusion, but what it comes down to is the manager and his subordinates' poor coordination of commitments. The marketing representatives could've clarified which of them would be responsible for various aspects of the report. The manager could've informed them why he needed the report, so they'd have been able to treat his request with the appropriate urgency and would've understood the kind of detail required. The manager also could've avoided a last-minute emergency if he'd checked the senior marketing reps' availability before committing to a specific time to meet with the executive.

This kind of poor coordination creates a lot of waste: work needs to be redone, redundant tasks are generated in different teams, important commitments "fall through the cracks" because everyone assumes someone else will do it. In the long run, miscoordination leads to poor customer satisfaction, longer response times, and missed opportunities. It has a ripple effect, endangering commitments and spreading waste beyond the immediate situation, too. For instance, while the senior reps in our example finally agreed to assist the manager, they could do so only at the expense of other commitments. Some other work no doubt had to be put off, with consequences for other internal or external customers. Outside of the workplace, the friends and family of all concerned are affected as well.

Miscoordination also has a more lasting and more damaging effect: it erodes the trust that's fundamental to relationships. If the manager's experience in the example above is repeated, he may lose confidence in his supporting team. For their part, the team may begin to resent the manager due to the extra work and the disruption in their personal lives. This can become a vicious cycle in which distrust and lack of open, clear communication leads to more miscoordination, and then to deeper distrust. Ultimately, this can result in an organization that is, in a sense, built around distrust. The company becomes full of rigid controls, checks, and procedures that attempt to force people to act responsibly, but which actually create further walls between people and bring effective action to a grinding halt.

Commitment and Language

How can people effectively intervene in this cycle of miscoordination and distrust and begin to reverse it? Let's look at the critical role of language. We often deemphasize the role of language in our lives and in our work. We've all heard "talk is cheap" and "it's easier said than done." But this common perception of language hides an important fact: language is our primary means for coordinating our activities. When you think about it, others in your firm only know what you're currently working on when you or someone else speaks to them about it. Language plays a crucial role in any shared enterprise and is essential for pursuing cooperative activities effectively.

When we speak, we're not just describing or talking about possible actions, we're acting: we're making things happen. This may seem like a trivial point, but it's important to understanding the central role language plays in action. When we speak, we make commitments to ourselves and to our listeners. These commitments create certain possibilities for action while simultaneously closing off others.

For example, suppose that a businesswoman needs a ride to the airport early the next morning. She asks her friend to drop her off; he agrees. Since the businesswoman asked her friend to take her to the airport and her friend agreed, each will act differently in the future. By agreeing, the friend will now spend the next morning preparing and taking the businesswoman to the airport. Other possibilities that might've been open to him are closed off: he can't sleep in, he can't have a leisurely breakfast at a cafe, he can't do other things that he might've previously planned to do. Similarly, the businesswoman will also act differently. Now she doesn't have to worry about getting to the airport, which means she doesn't have to spend more time looking for some other means of getting there because she knows that this small part of her future is being taken care of by someone she trusts.

In speaking and listening to each other, the businessperson and her friend take specific, observable actions that organize their subsequent expectations and activities. So we can see that *language and conversations aren't peripheral to action, but fundamental to it.* It is through language, the commitments we make in speaking, that we actually shape and create a common future. This may seem like a big claim relative to the example we've offered above, where the effects on the lives of the businesswoman and her friend are minimal. But the same is true for other commitments that we can more readily see as inventing our future. When a priest or judge pronounces a couple married, when an executive opens a new business or a new product line, when a president declares war on another nation: all of these are spoken actions that produce profound changes in the lives of many people.

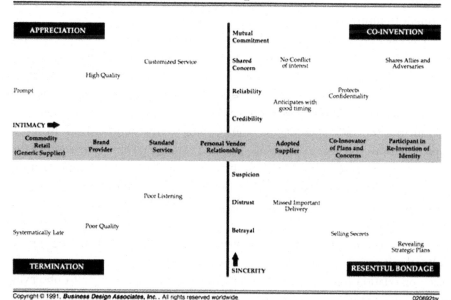

Trust in Customer Relationships BDA

From this perspective, making commitments, relying on others, granting trust to them, and striving to be trustworthy ourselves are all inescapable.

We do these things all the time. These are the capacities that constitute our lives together, that allow us to imagine and accomplish things greater than our own individual abilities. *The question is, how can we begin to observe and improve our habits for coordinating our commitments, making ourselves more trustworthy and more effective in furthering action for ourselves and others?*

Conversations for Action: Moves for Coordination

In chemistry, the periodic table details the natural elements' characteristics and outlines the possibilities opened up by their interactions. Similarly, the moves in what we call "conversation for action" each point to the various ways we can coordinate with others to create opportunities and bring them to fruition. Because we focus on language as we create and complete commitments, we're able to distinguish a relatively small set of observable actions and explore their importance in building trust and moving action forward in relationships, teams, and larger organizations. The basic actions are independent of language and culture, and they can be observed wherever people come together in a joint commitment to future action.

For example, consider a simple request, such as asking for a cup of tea. Just exactly how you ask for a cup of tea and the personal and cultural significance of the event are very different in the United States, in the Middle East, and in Japan. In the United States, it's just tea, you can get it anywhere, and it comes in a paper cup. In the Middle East, you may need to go to a cafe, and asking for tea may include the understanding that you're going to sit around and talk awhile. In Japan, the way you get tea can range from a vending machine to enacting a formal ceremony with deep cultural significance. But despite these important differences, there will be a way for you to ask for, and for another person to agree to a way to provide you with, the tea and for you to give thanks and let him or her know you're satisfied. In that sense, the actions of committing ourselves to action together are more basic and fundamental than the particular languages or cultural institutions that govern how these commitments show up in a particular place or relationship. By focusing on them, we can bring a rigor to observing and designing how people coordinate commitments in organizations that's been missing in management theory so far.

There are four important classes of distinctions that we'll discuss below:

1. Motivations: the concerns behind our actions and the conditions of satisfaction that we're trying to produce, or asking others to produce, to address those concerns;
2. Actions: the fundamental speech acts of declaration, request, offer, promise, and assertion;
3. Structure: the conversation for action (also called the action work flow) as a coherent set of commitments in which two people propose and complete some future action; and
4. Roles: the customer and the performer of a conversation for action.

The sections below show the different stages in a conversation for action. We describe the commitments that appear in each stage, the commitments that move the action along to the next stage, and the completion of the conversation. When people coordinate successfully in this conversation, action happens, trust is enhanced, and relationships are strengthened. When things break down, it's an opening for waste and distrust.

Preparation of Request

When a person makes a request in response to some concern that he or she has, three crucial things happen in his or her relationship with whomever is listening:

- he or she casts himself or her in a particular role—the role of customer—for this conversation;
- he or she casts the other person into the role of the performer; and
- he or she offers some initial interpretation of the **conditions of satisfaction** (more below);

that is, the kind of action or sequence of actions he or she wants to see happen to address his or her concern.

These two people may have been speculating idly or just chatting before, but the request creates a new kind of relationship and shifts the conversation into "action mode." For example, in our opening story, the executive made a request of the manager, and, in making this request, he not only expressed his desire to have a meeting, but when he said he wanted to receive an update on the progress of a company project, he made it clear that he was the customer.

In the simplest of cases, we have a concern, we make a request, and the start of the conversation is no more complicated than that. In many situations, though—especially business situations where requests may involve the action of whole divisions of an enterprise—we take time to clarify what we're concerned about and what kind of request we should make. During this preparation phase, the customer may make certain assessments about his concerns and his current situation that help to formulate the request more effectively. These may include:

- which problems are currently being experienced;
- which areas improvements can be made;
- what the potential opportunity is and the investment he's willing to make to capture it;
- what the urgency is (the time frame of the request);
- who might perform this request well, which might include discussions about who he trusts, who he believes is competent;
- who has the time and resources to take on such a commitment.

The executive in the story made the assessment that he wasn't well informed on the recently initiated project in the marketing department, and that's what prompted him to make his request. He decided that the best person who could provide that information was the manager of the marketing representatives, and therefore he directed the request to him.

If we look closely at the assessments that prompt a request, we see that these are assessments about how well our concerns are being taken care of. The executive had a concern about the marketing project's progress. Without this concern, his assessment that he wasn't well informed would be meaningless. If he didn't care about the project's progress, his recognition that he didn't know anything about the project would have no influence on his future actions. In preparing to make a request, we're listening to and reflecting our own concerns. In this respect, the simple act of making a request can be an occasion for learning.

Negotiation and Agreement

After a request is made, the customer and performer enter the negotiation stage. During this period, both parties discuss the terms of the request, including the time what was requested is to be delivered. The performer's own concerns and prior commitments and the urgency of the request need to be taken into account. The negotiation stage is ended by a promise on the performer's part to produce what was requested.

What the performer promises to do needn't be identical to what the customer initially requests—this is the point of the negotiation process. What is being negotiated are the customer's conditions of satisfaction, which may change depending on what happens in the discussion. If, for example, the performer has many previous commitments and cannot produce what the customer asked for in a given time frame, he can renegotiate a later deadline. Or perhaps he has nothing else on his schedule and offers to finish the job sooner. Perhaps his knowledge of what's available compels him to offer something new or better than what was originally requested.

For example, a manager asks his printing company representative to send someone out to fix the printer down the hall from his office, which isn't working optimally. But the rep knows that his firm is coming out with a bigger, better printer in a few weeks, so he offers to bring a prototype instead, so the manager can see whether the new machine would be a better fit.

Ultimately, the performer strives to take care of the customer's concerns. In part, this involves providing some service or product to the customer. However, there's more to this than simply listening carefully to what the customer says— his or her conditions of satisfaction—and providing whatever he or she asks. Sometimes when you do exactly as the customer asks, you find in the end he or she is not satisfied anyway. This happens because, as we said in the section about concerns, each of us has a limited background and set of experiences from which to view our concerns and problems.

It's not unusual that the customer's interpretation of his or her conditions of satisfaction changes as a result of a conversation with the performer. The important thing during the negotiation stage is listening to the customer's concerns and helping them to design the conditions of satisfaction that will best address those concerns. In negotiation, the customer and the performer become attuned to one another; the customer expresses his concerns in making the request and the performer explains his availability, competence, and knowledge of a particular area.

We mentioned earlier that each person, because of his or her unique background and capabilities, offers different interpretations of the same situation. In other words, each person offers insights into certain possibilities that another might be blind to. It's often the case that the performer, based on his or her competencies, can offer alternate ways of satisfying the customer's concerns that the customer wasn't even aware of. The performer could then offer the customer other possible conditions of satisfaction. In some instances, this results not only in a change of the initial request, but also in a new way of thinking about the customer's concerns. So we see here that a potential source of confusion and misunderstanding can also be a source for innovation.

Given the distinctions introduced thus far, we can already begin to see some of the coordination breakdowns in our story. After hearing the executive's request, the manager was too quick to promise to hold the meeting. He didn't take into consideration his prior commitments or the marketing representatives' prior commitments, despite the fact that they'd play a crucial role in helping him prepare for the meeting. Furthermore, the manager didn't discuss the concern behind his request, reducing the likelihood of that concern being satisfied and giving the marketing reps little or no ground to negotiate.

In many cases, the preparation and negotiation stages aren't explicitly carried out. The point of preparation and negotiation is to develop a shared understanding of the customer's concerns. For many simple requests, the customer and performer already share this understanding and it's not necessary to methodically go through the steps of preparation and negotiation. It would be tedious if every time you asked to borrow a pen, the other person asked what concerns you have in making that request. In many instances, though, spending more time listening and negotiating up front can eliminate a lot of wasted effort later on.

Performance and Declaration of Completion

Once the customer and performer agree on the conditions of satisfaction and the performer makes a promise, the future changes for both of them. As we showed in an earlier example, the promise creates an expectation in which the customer can feel comfortable that his concerns are being taken care of. He doesn't have to worry or spend additional time or resources finding alternate ways of satisfying his concern. The performer must budget his time and other commitments in order to deliver the conditions of satisfaction on time.

A promise opens up the performance stage of a conversation for action. During the performance stage, the performer produces the conditions of satisfaction. It's important that the performer stays in touch with the customer and other possible performers and promptly updates everyone involved on any unexpected changes or delays.

The performance stage is concluded when the performer assesses that he's fulfilled the request and makes a declaration of completion. A declaration is a speech act where we bring about precisely what we say. The most obvious examples of this phenomenon involve the use of institutional authority. For example, the CEO of a company may declare that someone will be the new vice president of marketing. From then on, the new vice president, as well as other people in and outside the organization, will act in accordance with that declaration. In the conversation for action, the performer declares, "I'm done!" and either presents or reports on whatever product, service, or actions he or she has agreed to produce.

Acceptance and Declaration of Satisfaction

With the performer's declaration of completion, there's a sense that "the work has been done." In our usual working habits, the conversation often stops here: "You asked for it, I did it, that's the end of it." From the perspective of the conversation for action, though, that isn't the end of the conversation. The performer's declaration of completion begins the acceptance stage of a conversation for action. The customer is no longer expecting something to happen at some future date; the time has arrived. At this point, the customer assesses how well what the performer delivered satisfies his concerns. The performer is no longer actively producing the conditions of satisfaction; now he or she is waiting for the customer's assessments. Once the customer assesses that his concerns have been taken care of, he makes a declaration of satisfaction. This declaration often comes in the form of a simple "thank you." A declaration of satisfaction completes the conversation for action.

On the other hand, what is produced may not be satisfactory, and in that case, the whole cycle starts all over again. Or the customer and performer may agree to end the conversation unresolved. In addition, for actions involving larger projects, the customer and performer may discuss both the successes and breakdowns that were experienced, new opportunities for working together, and how they can coordinate more effectively in the future. The customer and performer can use this stage as a platform for learning and strengthening their relationship.

Variations of Basic Moves

The conversations for action which we've outlined above, initiated either by a request or an offer, constitute complete conversations for action in their simplest form. Often, though, the world isn't so stable and predictable that we can't readily complete our commitments. In such cases, conversations for action may include a number of variations of the four basic moves. These variations on the four basic speech acts provide flexibility in managing our commitments when faced with unexpected changes.

For instance, if you're unable to fulfill the customer's request, you may decline to do so. Declining is a speech act that functions like a promise: you're committing yourself to not providing the requested conditions of satisfaction. Similarly, if you've already promised but are unable to fulfill, you may revoke your prior commitment. Although we typically don't like to do either, declining and revoking are important moves in coordinating action with others. When you fail to promptly decline or revoke, others may be counting on you and miss opportunities to find alternatives. Likewise, if a customer no longer needs what's been requested, he may cancel, and it's best to do so as soon as possible. It can be very frustrating to continue working and deliver on a promise, only to be told that the concern is no longer there or has been addressed in some other way.

There's a paradox in the habits many of us have for dealing with requests that causes a lot of waste and anxiety for people. We're afraid that declining and revoking promises will inconvenience other people and destroy their trust in us. But if we really can't deliver on the commitment on time or with the quality needed, this is going to happen anyway, and can be worse than we imagined.

Another possibility, both in the original negotiation and when problems arise, is to counteroffer. In a counteroffer, you decline to fulfill the customer's original request, but promise to provide other conditions of satisfaction. If we can decline or revoke and still take care of the customer's concerns—by offering to handle them at another time, offering something else, or putting them in touch with someone else who can help—we actually increase people's trust in us. A simple example is when we're looking for something in a store, and the person behind the counter has to say it's not in stock, but directs us to a competitor. That's a store we're going to return to again, because its service extends even beyond its own shelves and profits.

Finally, when you first receive a request, you may also commit to commit; that is, notify the customer that you can't commit now, but promise to give him or her a commitment later. Often when we receive a request, we feel that we're "on the spot" and have to commit right away one way or the other. This is an enormous source of hidden waste in our coordination, because often we make promises we really can't fulfill under this pressure, or miss opportunities out of an automatic sense that we "just have too much to do." By committing to commit, we can give ourselves a little breathing room to examine our own concerns, commitments, and priorities, and coordinate with other people who might be affected. Often we find that with a little conversation and renegotiation with other customers, we can take on a new commitment without adversely affecting other people. When we don't give ourselves this room, though, all kinds of waste happens: we have unclear priorities, we feel overwhelmed, and we start slipping on our commitments to others.

So far we have learned the basic moves of a conversation for action. In summary:

you declare something missing, declare the conditions under which you would be satisfied, and request that I fulfill your conditions of satisfaction.

- I promise to fulfill your request by a certain time.
- I report (declare) that I have fulfilled your request.
- You declare yourself satisfied or dissatisfied.

Each step is a commitment by a speaker; when commitments are taken together, they produce action. What was declared missing is no longer missing.

Conclusion

At the beginning of this chapter, we said that poor coordination is a major source of waste and dissatisfaction in our working lives and destroys the trust between people that's crucial for building strong working relationships internally and externally. In the current business environment, eliminating waste of all kinds and building stronger relationships with customers, allies, suppliers, and others is increasingly important. We cannot address these issues with good engineering alone. We have to recognize that the changes sweeping business today are not an anomaly. In some sense, these kinds of changes are the "natural order of things," because people always have concerns about the future and are always inventing new interpretations and ways to take care of those concerns. And people do this together, in language, by creating and completing new commitments.

We've offered a brief account of the discipline we've developed to illuminate the crucial role of language in effective action. The conversation for action is a kind of "design language" that allows us to both uncover a new source of waste and create more effective ways of working together.

CHAPTER 3

Conversations For Action And Workflow

As we saw in the previous essays, there are four distinct moments in a conversation of action: request/offer; promise/acceptance (which we also call agreement); declaration of completion; and declaration of satisfaction. These moments and their preceding phases are illustrated in the loop or workflow (see "Basic Action Workflow"). In this essay, we will elaborate on the practical implications of these distinctions for creating workflows and business processes.

Let's take a conversation between a business supervisor and a business consultant and move with it through the entire workflow:

Preparation -> Request: A business supervisor plans to present one of the new business offers developed in his area to his vice president and ultimately to the entire corporation for future sale to external customers. In order to prepare himself for a meeting with the vice president, he requests that his business consultant provide him with the necessary background information on the development of new business in their area within two days.

Negotiation -> Agreement: The business consultant already had a number of prior commitments to the business supervisor and doesn't see how she can manage to complete the report on time. She negotiates with the supervisor by counteroffering to submit the report to him within three days. This won't work for the supervisor, so he, in turn, counterrequests that she delay one of her other commitments in order to complete the new business report on time. The business consultant agrees to do so.

Again, notice that the future that is built in this exchange is mutual; it's not a one-sided commitment by either the business consultant or her manager. The compromise involves changes in the business consultant's schedule, including when and whether she completes other, previously planned projects. Likewise, the manager takes for granted that the report will get completed; he won't ask someone else to prepare the same report, or work on it himself.

If we don't take such a mutual commitment seriously, we might produce bad moods, breakdowns in our work, and possible damage in our work relationships. For example, the supervisor might get angry if the report isn't completed in time for his meeting, or the business consultant might get annoyed if she spends two days preparing a report that her supervisor files away and never uses. This kind of behavior not only produces immediate breakdowns for the business supervisor and the business consultant, but could also erode trust between the two of them, making them much less likely to accomplish successful work together in the future.

Performance -> Declaration of Completion: Now the business consultant gets to work: she interviews several CSRs and services and asks about their involvement in developing new business; she has an extensive phone conversation with the supervisor of new business development at Distribution Business Services (DBS) to get some advice from him; and she puts together a plan for designing the report. Finally, on the evening of the second day, she's compiled the report and leaves it on the business supervisor's desk.

Acceptance -> Declaration of Satisfaction: The next morning, the business supervisor finds the report on new business on his desk. He reads it, then sends the business consultant an e-mail message thanking her for the good work she's done. When she receives that message, the consultant is quite proud. The workflow is complete.

But what if the business supervisor is *not* satisfied with the report? In that case, the situation would look quite different: The next morning the business supervisor finds the report on his desk. After reading it, he calls the business consultant to his office and tells her that she didn't include the potential profitability margins for the newly developed product in the report. Without those figures, his proposal to the vice president would lack credibility, he tells her. Before leaving to go to rework the report, the business consultant makes sure that all other items in the report are to the supervisor's satisfaction. As you can see, they went back to the negotiation phase to clarify the conditions of satisfaction. After coming to agreement again, the business consultant adds the missing figures to the report, and then returns it to the supervisor. He thanks her for the changes and then sits down to prepare himself for his meeting with the vice president.

Basic Action Workflow

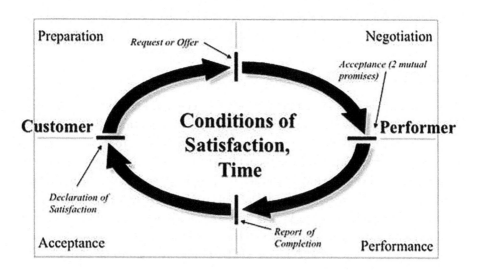

From Workflow to Business Process

We can look at the workflow as a simple transaction between two parties—the customer and the performer. It constitutes the basic unit in a network of workflows that we call a business process. All action that happens in business starts with either an offer by a performer or a request by a customer somewhere in this network. In our example regarding the development of new business, we could identify a business process with the following loops:

- Make new service offer to residential customers.
- Invent and design new service offers.

- Prepare report on status of new business development.
- Make presentation of business case to vice president for approval.
- Develop and implement new service offer.
- Test customer satisfaction regarding the new service offer.

Looking at business processes this way helps us identify areas where we encounter breakdowns in our work. These breakdowns could be based on missing conditions of satisfaction, confusion about who the customer or the performer is, missing phases in the workflow, duplication of loops, and so forth. The workflow then becomes a useful tool for observing and redesigning the way we work together.

Business Process Design

In identifying the various distinctions of a conversation for action or workflow, let's remind ourselves that we do this for the sake of observing what we produce in speaking with each other. The purpose of introducing you to these distinctions isn't for you to memorize or learn them like a laundry list, but rather to open your horizons to observing the moves you and the people around you make in speaking. Observing these distinctions in language will enable you to take new and different actions with the people at work. And then we can begin to alter, modify, or even totally change how we do business with our co-workers and our customers.

In order to follow through on the kinds of offers we can invent with this type of listening, we need a way to rapidly reconfigure the business processes of our own companies. Our interpretation of business process design is based on the workflow "atoms" that we presented above in our discussion of coordination of action. In distinguishing this simple set of primitives for cooperative work, we are doing much more than giving people a different way of thinking about their jobs. We are also laying the foundation of a discipline for observing the "soft processes" in business that have resisted traditional approaches to business analysis and design. The processes typically considered "soft"—such as the coordination between people and unstructured work—are now becoming the focus of competitive advantage. Significant opportunities are opening up for people who can manage these processes with the same rigor applied to manufacturing. As we've developed our work on these topics in great detail elsewhere, we are only going to touch on them briefly.

In the accompanying chart, "Types of Processes," we present three different ways of looking at the processes that make up a business. The earliest tradition interprets business as what we call a material process: a sequence of physical actions (movement, storage, transformation, etc.) that are performed on raw materials to produce finished products. The fields of industrial and mechanical engineering have long provided the foundation for analyzing and improving the productivity of these processes in manufacturing. More recently, the widespread use of computers in business has resulted in a concern for managing data and the company's information processes. Just as material processes manipulate physical objects, information processes are viewed as sequences of actions that manipulate information. These processes may include moving, storing, comparing, and transforming information about customers, transactions, inventory, financial performance, and so on. In response to this need, new disciplines have arisen, such as computer-assisted software engineering and information technology design.

Material and information processes have proved themselves beneficial for understanding business situations that are structured, specifiable, and repeatable. However, they have not provided the same benefits for analyzing the often unstructured and unique interactions of the "human side" of work. With the workflow structure that we presented earlier, we can apply an equivalent rigor to the observation of a third kind of process, the business process. Rather than tracking the flow of materials or data, business processes chart the coordination of action between people (and sometimes machines) involved in an activity.

Interpreting business processes in this way doesn't challenge the existing traditions of material and information processes. Instead, it complements them by adding a third perspective. Material processes allow us to design the flow of materials on an assembly line or in an office. Information processes allow us to design the movement of data within an organization. Likewise, business processes allow us to design the coordination and flow of commitments that lead to customer satisfaction. There is, however, a sense in which business processes are senior to the other two types, for these two types of processes are always triggered by the commitments represented in business processes. No order entry process is going to start without a customer request, and no car will roll off the line without the promises written into a production schedule.

Since business processes provide a means of observing a company's coordination at this basic level, they also provide a set of principles for process analysis and reengineering that's independent of any particular business or any future changes in technology. Furthermore, the same few primitive distinctions for observing business processes can be applied uniformly to any part of the business. From the standpoint of workflow structure, there's little difference between the CEO requesting strategic directions from a company's executives and a customer asking a service representative for help in installing a new software package.

This last point presents a new and dramatic possibility: that we can learn to design an entire business with as much rigor as we use in configuring a computer network or production line. Not only that, but any design that used the principles we have presented here would be built from the very start around customer satisfaction. We expect that if such a practice were to become commonplace, it would generate new tools, new skills, and new ways to create and manage competitive enterprises.

Type of Process	Purpose	Structure & Elements	Examples
Business Process	Satisfy customers, complete offers and requests, satisfy stakeholders, accommodate custom requests	Workflows Roles Conditions of satisfaction Time	-Completing transaction and producing satisfaction when a customer requests a product or service, or a company offers a product -Sales order triggers transactions with inventory, manufacturing, and distribution to fulfill
Information Process	Assemble data into information products, i.e., inscriptions and records used to support acts taken in material or business process.	Documents and records, data storage and retrieval, transmissions, manipulation, assembly, and comparison	-Order data entered into a database, computer transactions for financial transactions, processing of invoices, information systems
Material Process	Assemble components into product unities	Product unites raw materials transportation, storage, assembly, transformation, and comparison against standards.	-Movement of paper in office, manufacturing products in assembly lines, distributing and delivery of products

CHAPTER 4

Conversations For Possibilities

L et's pause for a moment and ask some questions about how to get to action. Let's consider the conversations in which possibilities for action are declared, because you make requests and promises after you have these kinds of conversations. While you're working, you're not "thinking about what you're doing;" you're making requests, proposals, invitations, and promises; asking questions; declining requests; finding telephone numbers; and locating people, among many other things. You're "doing." Questions like "Where am I headed?" and "Is this the place I want to be headed?" aren't central in your consciousness. Where *are* you headed, then?

The answer is simple: you're headed where you're headed, as fast as you can get there. Let's discuss all that later; now, there's work to do.

But before you "went into action," you had a conversation that framed your actions, whether you noticed it or not. At some point, you decided to move in a specific direction. Unfortunately, the "conversation" before your conversations for action is almost never handled well.

Yet how well you accomplish this framing conversation later determines whether you've been working on a relevant opportunity or you've been wasting your time. What happens in this conversation "before" is that you declare that some possibility can be fulfilled if you head in a particular direction. Therefore, that's where you're headed.

We call the kind of conversation in which you declare a possibility a "conversation for possibilities." In this type of conversation, you declare a domain in which you will invent and fulfill opportunities with conversations for action. These conversations are very different from those for action. Conversations for possibilities lead to and are completed by conversations for action.

Inventing Conversations for Possibilities

Although conversations for possibilities are the most common kind of human conversation, they are perhaps the least well examined. People are engaged in conversations for possibilities all the time, without any awareness that these conversations are under way and "out of control." Let's analyze a few examples.

Someone says, "Rotten day, isn't it?" What this little speech normally means is, "I declare that a lot is not possible today, certainly not as much as is possible on an 'average' day, and I invite you to join me in that declaration." Although that's a trivial example of a conversation for negative possibilities, it illustrates how pervasive these conversations for possibilities are. Here's another example: Someone says, "I think we might be able to create a new business by talking to these people differently than they're used to." In this case, we have a classic move in a conversation for possibilities — a declaration of a new possibility, simultaneously bringing forth and framing the possibility by the mere mention of it.

Please notice that we're not offering a new or better way of *planning* your actions. The kind of work we're considering isn't "planning." Sometimes people doing planning aspire to raise the questions we raise, but we're actually *creating* by declaring the possibilities in some domain, and that's not planning. Nor are we saying that planning is irrelevant, but it does become simpler when you're clear about the possibilities.

According to conventional wisdom, it becomes easier to act and actions are clearer when they're "planned from the beginning." But effective action can't be planned from the beginning unless it's the kind of action a machine can carry out. The kind of action human beings are uniquely qualified to do—to bring forth what's missing—can't be "planned from the beginning." Action emerges from committed interactions of people making requests and promises in networks of commitments; such networks aren't brought forth by plans.

On the other hand, acting becomes simpler and the "right" kinds of requests, invitations, offers, proposals, etc., appear by themselves when the possibility you seek to fulfill is clear. For example, let's imagine a CEO whose company is doing well, but that needs to offer new lines of business to continue its current rate of growth. Imagine that he gathers the best and the brightest of his executives and asks them to brainstorm some new product ideas. What else can we do with our current people, processes, and plants, he asks them? What else can we make or what service can we offer that our customers need and would buy? Now imagine he asks those same executives for some "plans" for new products.

The brainstorming session brings to mind some top-notch talent, who stand shoulder deep in that firm's culture and operations, coming up with some new products using already trained people, processes they know well, in plants they already know and trust. The "plans" request brings to mind committees, busywork, and little action.

Basic Elements

The basic elements of conversations for possibilities are described briefly below. With practice, you can develop a permanent discipline of engaging in conversations for possibilities, so that the possibilities you pursue in life are *your* possibilities rather than simply those that happen to come to you.

The central feature of conversations for possibilities is the conversations you have with yourself and with others in which you declare things like the kind of person you are, the roles you're willing to play, the family and relationships you will have, the career you'll follow, the projects you'll undertake, and what will work for you. Thus, in conversations for possibilities, you produce the domains in which you have conversations for action, undertake specific actions to make possibilities real, and complete possibilities.

The first essential element of a conversation for possibilities is the declaration of a break.

You may say to yourself, "But wait a moment here." Or, you may say many other things. The essence is, "I declare a break for myself in this matter, and I declare that I need to engage in a conversation for possibilities."

The second essential, to be spoken repeatedly during this conversation, is the declaration of the possibility itself.

Perhaps what's possible will appear as a series of declarations that begin as musings and end as strong pronouncements:

"I wonder if…"

"I think it's possible that…"

"I'm beginning to be certain that…"

"I'm sure that…"

"That's what we'll do!"

At the end of the conversation for possibilities, at the moment of transition to conversations for action, this declaration will often appear as a formal announcement:

"We are pleased to announce that our company has embarked on a new program…." The movement from musing to strong pronouncement is accomplished through these other elements of the conversation:

Specifying the actions possible in the declared domain of possibility.

Declaring new possibilities opened by the conversation.

CHAPTER 5

Assertions And Assessments

The previous chapters have focused on conversations for getting work done, for making things happen. We coordinate our work through conversations for action; we invent the work to be done through conversations for possibilities. In this chapter, we'll introduce additional concepts that are crucial for making things happen.

When we work on projects with others, we're constantly assessing their work and they, ours. Most people find accepting and making assessments difficult. In fact, many projects fail to achieve completion for this very reason. Revising or renegotiating conditions of satisfaction requires that people be capable of making assessments about the work performed. In addition, we must make assessments about the future we see possible. Making assessments about the future, we will see, does not produce the same type of stress as does trying to predict to the future. People struggle with decision making as they try to predict the future, rather than make assessments about the future.

In this chapter, we'll show how assessments are a type of declaration that can be grounded or ungrounded. Assessments are declarations about what kinds of possibilities for action are opened and closed for us in the future. The challenge for most of us is that we tend to confuse assessments with assertions, which are distinctions about observable facts in the world. To understand the previous claim, let us first look at our common notion of information.

41

What Is Information?

Today we take information so much for granted that this might seem like a silly question. Our traditional understanding of information is so deep-seated that it seems like information is just common sense. Information is a collection of objective facts about the world. When we make decisions, we use information to determine the future consequences of all the alternative actions we might take, and choose the action with the best projected outcome.

But information isn't just a set of facts, because all information is ultimately derived from assertions about the world made by individual people. And people don't make these assertions from a detached and objective perspective; they have different concerns and backgrounds of experience, and they make assertions to support some future action. Making a decision isn't a simple matter of choosing among predetermined outcomes. Instead, we create the future in assessments that are both interpretations of emerging possibilities and commitments to a course of action for coping with and exploiting those possibilities.

This interpretation avoids several pitfalls in the traditional view of information. When the information we've gathered is seen as the "truth" about the world, independent of particular observers or circumstances, we can become closed to the different interpretations that others might offer, and to courses of action that we might not have considered ourselves. Or if we do try to cover all the bases, we may end up endlessly gathering information and never reaching a resolution. Even worse, our "objective" analysis of the situation may suggest to us that no action is possible; nothing will change or improve the situation.

In all of these cases, our traditional ways of evaluating information—looking for objective truth and completeness—can undermine rather than support our need to take action. The new interpretation we're proposing holds effective action as its most central concern and most relevant standard for judging information.

The Paradigm of Information and Decision Making

Our traditional understanding of information is based on the twin notions of objectivity and accuracy. This paradigm's foundational assumption is that there's an objective "natural order" to reality, and it's possible to judge people's statements about the world as true or false independent of their particular concerns, interpretations, or circumstances. Under this view, "good" information consists of a set of facts that match reality, providing a source of reliable forecasts about the future. "Bad" information doesn't match reality and, along with lack of information, is the source of poor forecasts and bad decisions.

The set of theoretical assumptions of the decision-making paradigm influential in management science and other disciplines is, *if we could only have access to all of the relevant, accurate facts and enough computing power, we could have a perfect model of the future and we'd always make the most rational decisions.* Good decisions are made when people lay out all possible courses of action, calculate all the consequences of each, and choose the action with the best consequences. This view posits that only a lack of sufficient factual information and/or a lack of time for adequate analysis stand between us and perfectly rational decision making and action.

The situation isn't quite so simple. When we assume that information is objective, we forget that information doesn't create itself. Our capacity to predict the future isn't limited only by the sheer volume of the information we gather, but also by the fact that all information is derived from the observations of particular people with their own individual concerns and experiences. The range of perspectives one can have on a situation is infinite, and no observer has either the capacity or the interest to "tell the whole story."

So we can never predict the future accurately because there's no possibility of a source or analyzer of information free from interpretation. Failing to observe this phenomenon leads to all the breakdowns mentioned in the introduction. Believing your information is truth can blind you to different interpretations and possibilities. On the other hand, trying to be open to all possibilities by gathering all the information you can find will lead to information overload and paralysis. Too much faith in unexamined "facts" can lead to a situation in which all the information suggests there's no hope, no possibility for action—the most useless interpretation of all. This last point reflects the very heart of the problem. In the traditional paradigm, we can get so caught up in the accuracy of our information and the completeness of our predictions that we lose sight of the whole point of making decisions: taking action.

Assertions and Assessments

The very concept of information makes sense only in the context of human action. We're constantly involved in conversations with other people, coordinating our actions to bring about some future **possibility** to which we're all mutually committed. And in these conversations, we can distinguish not one sense of information (true-false), but two conversational moves: assertions and assessments. *(The structure of these moves is presented at the end of this chapter).* We use the phrase "conversational move" here to emphasize that *when people make assertions and assessments, they're not transmitting information from one mind to another; they're making commitments to each other about how to coordinate their actions.*

In making an assertion, a person supplies the answer to a question. For example, a sales manager may be trying to decide who to put in charge of a major new account. In the process, he may ask one of the senior salespeople, "Has Dave completed all his client calls for this month?" She answers him with the assertion, "Well, Dave hasn't returned three client calls in the last two weeks."

Note that the actual question isn't so important here. What *is* important is that in making an assertion, the speaker provides the hearer with something he or she needs in order to take further action.

Because the hearer is going to rely on the assertion, there's a certain amount of commitment involved on the speaker's part. For instance, the speaker of an assertion commits himself or herself to providing further evidence to support his or her initial statement. The sales manager may ask, "How do you know this?" which prompts another assertion from the salesperson: "June told me he missed a call last Thursday and two so far this week."

Another aspect is that an assertion must not be mere speculation, but something that's suitable as a basis for future action. An assertion must involve a recognized distinction, a past action, or an event that's potentially observable by anyone. In this sense, an assertion can be either true or false, given a community with common distinctions and standards for observation. For example, the statement, "I don't know, Dave seems kind of flaky to me" isn't an assertion in our interpretation; "flakiness" is a characterization that may have an infinite number of interpretations. Note again that it's not so important that the person making the assertion witnessed the action himself. What *is* critical is that the hearer accepts the speaker's standards for reliable observation. In our present example, the manager may accept hearsay evidence from a reliable source,

44

saying, "Well, if June says he's been missing calls, then I guess we ought to be concerned."

Unlike an assertion, an assessment can never be directly witnessed. Assessments are verdicts, as in the characterization of Dave as "flaky." In making an assessment, the essential commitment is about the course of action a person or community will take in the future. To the extent that other people accept the salesperson's characterization of Dave, they'll cease to rely on him for important tasks. An assessment, then, is a kind of declaration in which future possibilities aren't simply predicted, they're actually created. This is easier to see when the person making the assessment is in a position of authority. Suppose that the sales manager accepted his subordinates' assertions and said, "I guess Dave isn't reliable enough for that account." Unless someone challenges this assessment with a different interpretation, it's clear to all participants in the meeting that Dave will not be on that team.

Although an assessment can't be true (directly observable) or false in the sense that an assertion can, it can be what we call grounded or ungrounded. The central characteristic of a grounded assessment is that it's limited to a particular domain of concern in which a person or community can take action. Given that the point of making an assessment is reaching some resolution about what action to take next, that isn't surprising, With just this initial point, we can see that our earlier example, "Dave seems kind of flaky to me" is an ungrounded assessment. It's not limited to any domain of action, and so it only provides a very shallow stereotype of Dave. If someone accepted this characterization of him, they'd be in a permanent mood of distrusting his competence at anything, which isn't exactly a productive working relationship.

A grounded assessment is also supported by a collection of assertions about the past that suggest a systematic pattern, not just a single coincidental observation. In our example, the salesperson was able to offer three separate assertions about Dave's past performance that could ground her manager's assessment of Dave. If she'd mentioned only one incident and the manager made the same assessment, we'd be likely to say that he was doing so out of bias or his personal opinion about Dave.

Finally, we cannot judge whether an assessment is grounded unless we've shared standards for how many and what kinds of assertions we will accept as evidence. We may imagine that all of the people in our fictional meeting feel that dropping three calls in two weeks is unacceptable performance, but we can also easily imagine that there's no explicit agreement on this standard among the team members, most crucially including Dave. When we're trying to move a community of people to action, it's critical that the standards for assessing satisfactory performance are clearly articulated and shared by all community members.

Speech Acts Review Part 2

Speech Act	Action	Required Elements	Examples	What Is Produced
Assess	A speaker assesses how some action or thing relates to specific concerns or commitments.	• Making a verdict (verdictive family of declarations). • Can be grounded or ungrounded (never true or false). • For grounding: • for the sake of what are you making this assessment (what is your concern for the future)? • Hypothesis of recurrence. • Standards upon which you base your verdict.	"We are in a mature industry." "Our customers are not happy." "John is impatient." "Our costs are increasing too much."	Preparation for action: Orientation, interpretations, and attitudes toward actions or situations.

Assert	A speaker reports facts pertinent to the concern at hand.	• Answers a question of the listener— spoken or unspoken. • Includes an implicit offer to provide evidence. • Evidence can be witnessed and community accepts evidence. • Can be true or false.	"The meeting was at 4 p.m. PST." "The gauge reads 200 psi." "Our sales were $4.2 million last quarter."	-Confidence that we share a reliable and observable basis for our interpretation of the situation.

Ungrounded Assessments and Resignation

Given that assessments are declarations about what kinds of possibilities for action are opened and closed for us in the future, there's one particular class of assessments that should ring warning bells. **When someone makes the assessment that there's no action to be taken toward some concern, and no hope of the situation changing in the future, we say that they're stuck in resignation in that domain.** We've all noticed that a person who's resigned fails to see possibilities for action that are as plain as day to other observers, indicating that, for the most part, assessments that lead to resignation are inherently ungrounded. For example, people generalize across domains of concern, using few assertions, saying that because they once failed a high-school algebra class they'll "never be good at math." Learning to distinguish and examine the grounding of assessments can thus be a powerful tool for rooting out areas in which resignation is limiting our possibilities in life.

Objectivity and Action

Now that we've distinguished the phenomena of assertions and assessments and brought action back to the center of our concern in gathering information, we're able to appreciate the ways that information can be objective. One of the most compelling aspects of a traditional understanding of how the world works is a strong intuition that everything isn't relative to individual interpretation. We endorse that intuition. But we also soundly reject the notion that the only alternative to an objective "natural order" is some kind of fuzzy-headed relativism in which individual interpretations, no matter how bizarre, are all equally valid.

The answer to this dilemma is clear when we realize that human beings are social and historical beings who create the future together via action. The criteria for objectivity, then, are social. Recurrent effectiveness in bringing forth action, historical tradition, and the existence of a community with shared standards are sources of a kind of objectivity that, while not absolute truth, provide a means of distinguishing "good" and "bad" assertions and assessments. Grounded assessments can produce the results that good decision making was supposed to provide, without the pitfalls of looking at information as the "truth" about the world. They allow us to take effective action in a way that's more flexible and open to other interpretations, without the paralysis of resignation or the endless search for a perfect decision.

Assessment Delivery Exercise

This exercise consists of two roles, a recipient *and a* contributor. *The* contributor *makes an assessment; the* recipient *receives it. This exercise presumes a previous team agreement to give and receive assessments* for the sake of developing effective teamwork. *It also requires a minimal level of trust.*

Contributor: *(Say their name),* **I have an assessment for you. Is now a good time to give it you?**
Recipient: *(Settle and respond)* **Yes** or **No.**
If no, say when you'd like to talk. If yes, continue.
Contributor: **My assessment is** (make the assessment)**...and the reason I say that is...**(give your grounding; assertions (facts) are most effective for revealing your standards).
Recipient: **Thank you for making the assessment.**
Contributor: **You're welcome.**

Options

Clarification:

Recipient: **I'd like to discuss this further with you.** *(You could have questions about the grounding of the assessment. What assertions does the person have in support of the assessment? What concerns are behind the assessment?)*

Negative assessment:
Recipient: **Do you have any suggestions about what I can do to shift your assessment and hence make a stronger contribution to our team?**

Positive assessment:
Recipient: **Do you have any suggestions about what I can do to capitalize on this assessment and hence make a stronger contribution to our team?**

No action:
Recipient: **I'll consider what you said. Thank you.**
Note: As you complete this exercise, please reflect on your mood. If the recipient is in a negative mood, this may indicate that there are additional conversations to explore.

Fundamental Elements of an Assessment

The act of assessing requires that all the following elements appear in the listening of the relevant parties:

- Speaker commits him- or herself to a verdict (can be about a person, a group, an event, an object, etc.).
- An assessment can be grounded or ungrounded, but never true or false.

To be grounded, an assessment requires the following additional elements:

- The speaker is clear about the concern for which he or she is making the assessment.
- This concern limits the domain of the assessment.

- The speaker can articulate the standards he or she is using to make the assessment.
- The speaker can provide assertions to support the assessment.
- The speaker can present a hypothesis of recurrent evidence to support using the past to anticipate the future.

Fundamental Elements of an Assertion

The act of asserting requires that each the following elements appear in the listening of the relevant parties:

- Speaker commits him- or herself that x is true.
- Speaker includes an implicit offer to provide evidence.
- The assertion answers a question of the hearer's, either spoken or unspoken.
- It can be judged true or false by the hearer.
- It is sincere.

PART 2

Building Commitment

CHAPTER 6

Characterizations And Conversations For Moving Forward

Understanding how to make well-grounded assessments allows us to give and receive "opinions" from others not just about work, but about ourselves, our personalities. When getting work done, we find ourselves in situations where we assess other people as certain types, and they do the same with us. These types of assessments are characterizations; we always characterize other people. We classify people as intelligent, naive, funny, arrogant, and so forth. When we make these judgments, we start any new interaction with certain expectations. We anticipate that an "intelligent" person will say interesting and useful things, and that an "arrogant" person will be difficult to work with.

We also characterize ourselves. In conversations with ourselves and with others, we describe our faults and strengths. We do it in social situations when we talk about ourselves; we do it when we blame or praise ourselves. Examples: we say that we won an account because we're creative; we wrecked the car because we're careless; we didn't get a promotion because we're lazy. Based on these personal attributes, we expect to encounter similar successes and mistakes in the future.

We tend to forget that making a characterization is a conversation. To identify someone as intelligent or lazy doesn't identify permanent features of his or her personality. These "features" aren't real; they only exist in conversation. The danger of characterization is that assuming it *is* real may limit our possibilities. Yet making characterizations can locate potential areas for dealing with breakdowns that occur repeatedly. We can use them to develop concrete opportunities for ourselves.

Let's begin with explaining how making certain types of characterizations can limit our possibilities. For instance, if I say I'm reliable, I claim that I always act reliably (allowing that there will be exceptions), that I possess "reliability." I'll fulfill a promise or cancel it if I cannot keep it. I claim that this will always be so, that acting this way is a permanent feature of my personality or identity. Now this is not entirely true, because we cannot possibly know how we or anyone else will *always* act. But we make these characterizations anyway.

We also use characterizations to shut off opportunities with other people— "He's too dumb, arrogant, dishonest"—or with ourselves—"I'm too lazy, stupid, undisciplined." We produce excuses that make it impossible for us to ever act competently: "I just can't keep my checkbook balanced. I'm bad with numbers." Such characterizations destroy our capacity to act. They also destroy our capacity to change how we act, or to become competent in areas in which we are currently incompetent. Characterizing ourselves as "bad with numbers" condemns us to an eternity of numerical incompetence. We can do nothing about it.

When we forget that characterization is a conversation, we perpetuate our competencies and incompetencies, and those of others. But we can reconstruct a conversation of characterization to determine what we've forgotten. This enables us to see the positive role of characterizations, especially those that are "well grounded." Typically, our characterizations are not well grounded. These characterizations are the most damaging to our future and to our relationships. Grounded characterizations allow us to have productive conversations; these are conversations for moving forward together rather than staying stuck in the present.

Let's return to the example of calling someone reliable. What are we doing when we characterize someone as reliable? First, we're saying something about the past. A reliable person has, on particular occasions, fulfilled promises. He or she has rarely let a promise go without either fulfilling or canceling it. If our characterization is well grounded, we can offer such assertions about his or her past actions.

Second, to say that someone is reliable is to talk about his or her actions in a particular domain. With a domain, we distinguish and name a collection of actions. If our characterization is confined to the domain of social engagements, it could include "going to the movies," "meeting for dinner," "going to parties." We may have observed a person's actions in only one domain. Or perhaps we've observed him acting reliably in one domain and unreliably in others—e.g., in business promises or those concerning money. We confine our characterization to domains in which we can provide assertions about his actions. If we cannot supply assertions about his actions in the domain of business, we have no "grounds" to characterize him vis-à-vis business. If we can supply assertions about the person's actions in the domain of social engagements, we can ground characterizations in that domain.

Third, to say that someone is reliable is to speculate that she will act in the future as she's acted in the past. We commit to such speculation about the future whenever we make a "characterization."

Typically, we make these assessments about the future without offering evidence. We generalize permanent characteristics from only a few instances. If someone has once or twice failed to keep a promise, we say that he's unreliable, making it virtually a permanent pronouncement on his personality. We usually fail to confine our characterizations to particular domains of action. If I fail a class in mathematics, I might characterize myself as dumb in all domains, which generalizes my incompetence in one domain to a permanent trait that will appear in all kinds of actions. We forget we're speculating, and assume that we've nailed down a trait that will always cause a person to act as he or she does. This is what a characterization typically is for us: a permanent description of what a person can and cannot do.

In contrast, well-grounded characterizations can alert us to domains in which to anticipate breakdowns and opportunities in the future. For example, if I characterize myself as careless in the domain of personal finance, I identify a domain for future concern. If I do nothing about my carelessness, I speculate that I'll repeat what has occurred before—overdrawing my checking account or buying things I don't use.

But I can also use my characterization to prompt myself to action. I can resolve to balance my checkbook every day or to consider the real utility of something before I buy it. Perhaps I can enroll in a course in personal finance. I can take action to become competent in a domain in which I now regard myself as incompetent.

Positive characterizations can play a similar role. If I characterize myself as clever in the domain of investment, I can begin to listen to new opportunities there. I might consider particular new investments, or devote more time to earn a living this way. I may even take up investment or investment advising as a career.

The last two cases are self-characterizations. But we can make the same points concerning characterizations of ourselves that we hear from others. If theirs are well grounded, they highlight domains for concern as well as opportunities.

The key is to see characterization as a conversation. To forget this is to suppose that people have features that we can describe and nail down forever. Incompetencies become incompetencies forever, and all we can do is suffer with them. If we remember that characterization is a conversation, we can regard characterizations as signals to possible breakdowns and as prompts for action to become competent where we are not.

Observing and Analyzing Typical Characterizations

A characterization is well grounded when:

- You supply assertions about specific actions that a person has repeated several times in the past;
- You confine your characterization to a domain of verifiable actions;
- You're aware that your characterization also speculates about how that person will act in the future. You're not certain of this; you can only anticipate, given your assertions about his or her performance in the past.

Consider examples of two particular characterizations, "smart" and "dumb," to see how they appear in typical characterizations. The idea is to enable you to make characterization a way of opening opportunities to increase your and others' competencies rather than making your present competencies and incompetencies permanent.

Say that you're considering buying a new car and you go to a showroom. The cars you see all have what you call "complicated" instruments—many buttons, switches, and slide controls. You say to yourself, "I can't imagine what all those controls are for. I can't buy a car like this. I'm too dumb to ever learn how to drive it." You just characterized yourself as dumb. What does that mean in typical characterizations and the typical understanding of characterizations? It means you have a quality—let's call it "dumbness"—that's a permanent feature. It prevents you from doing, or forever learning to do, certain sorts of things.

Such a declaration about yourself comes from a conversation. You say to yourself, "This is just like when I was sixteen and I couldn't learn to operate the manual transmission in my father's car. The first time I drove it, I stalled the car five times. I'm just too dumb to ever do anything complicated."

What happened? What can we say when looking at the conversation, armed with our distinction of a typical characterization versus a well-grounded characterization? We can employ our distinctions for well-grounded characterization to ask whether this characterization is well grounded.

Have you supplied assertions about your specific actions over and over in the past?

We've cited one previous incident: when you were sixteen, something similar happened. You've not located your characterization in assertions about repeated actions in the past; you've generalized from only one action.

Have you confined your characterization to a domain of past actions about which you can supply assertions? No, you haven't. You've characterized yourself as "dumb" by saying, "I'm too dumb to ever do anything complicated." Your assertion about the past concerned operating a car, but the domain in which you claim to be dumb is much larger. It includes any "complicated action," such as solving mathematical problems, playing the piano, building model airplanes. You've generalized again from a domain of actions about which you can provide assertions to a much larger domain.

Were you aware that you were speculating about your actions in the future? You said, "I'm too dumb to ever do anything complicated." In saying this, you claimed something about the future; you claimed that something would never happen. You didn't say, "If things go on as they have, I don't anticipate ever doing anything complicated." Instead, you simply stated that it would never happen, as if it were a fact. Indeed, you weren't aware that you were speculating.

What do you produce with such generalizations and this sort of certainty about the future? You produce your own permanent incompetence over the domain you call "complicated" actions.

Let's try the same with the characterization "smart." You've just returned from a one-month intensive course in basic management skills. You scored more points than anyone else in the course on the final exam. As a result, you characterize yourself as "smart."

Again, what is your conversation—the conversation in which you characterize yourself this way? "I had the highest score. At work, I'm always the guy who solves the problem. I'm smarter than the other guys, and I'm going to be the one that sees what to do and how to do it."

Now, the same questions:

Have you supplied assertions about your specific actions over and over in the past?

You supplied only one assertion about specific actions in the past. You scored highest in the recent intensive course. You added a general claim, "I'm always the guy who solves the problem," without citing any specific actions or occasions. Again, you have generalized a permanent quality—"I'm smarter." In your characterization, you lose sight of how few assertions you can supply; you leap to a general conclusion about all of your performance in life up to the present.

Have you confined your characterization to a domain of past actions about which you can supply assertions? In your conversation, you distinguished no domain at all. You said, "I'm smarter than the other guys." You made no distinction of domains at all, no distinction about the kinds of actions for which your characterization was valid. You generalized your characterization from the few actions you cited to all distinguishable actions in any domain.

Were you aware that you were speculating about your actions in the future? You said, "I'm going to be the one that sees what to do and how to do it." Again, you said something about the future with the certainty of observable fact. You weren't aware that what you saw did not yet exist, but was only a speculation, something you could only anticipate without certainty.

In characterizing yourself as dumb, clearly, you closed off your own possibilities. You pronounced yourself forever incompetent for anything you call "complicated." Just as important, your characterization of yourself as smart also closed off possibilities. You pronounced yourself forever competent—more competent than others—without specifying any particular domain of actions in which you're competent. You closed off the possibilities of recognizing your own incompetencies, and of taking action to make yourself competent where you're now incompetent. In short, you closed off the possibility of learning from other people.

The mistake is in failing to see that characterizing yourself is a matter of talking about yourself. It's not a matter of discovering the qualities that have been there and always will be, because no such permanent qualities exist. There are only conversations in which you characterize yourself.

Characterizations and Standards

Characterizations are always relative to some standard. In assessing an action as "ineffective," we produce a standard of effectiveness that we say we've not attained. Our actions fail to "measure up." The problem is, usually such standards aren't explicit. We may be hard pressed to formulate them if asked to do so.

Let's go back to our example of "unreliability." We characterize ourselves as unreliable after observing our actions in the domain we call money. We assess our actions as ineffective since we've failed in several actions. We've not paid the phone bill on time in the last five months; we've paid the rent late in six of the last ten months. And we're overdue in returning one hundred dollars we borrowed from a friend.

What is our standard of effectiveness for assessments of our own actions? We say that effectiveness in paying debts is to pay in full and on time. When we don't meet those standards, our actions are ineffective. Notice that our standards for effective action aren't a matter of individual choice. We learn them from living with and talking with other people. Shared standards are essential for coordinating our actions with others.

What's lacking when we fail to meet these standards isn't the quality of reliability; what's lacking is taking action to meet our standards of effectiveness. This interpretation changes what we can do about our negative characterization. To become reliable, we need to take certain actions. In this case, it means paying bills and repaying debts in full and on time.

Where We Can't Simply Take Action

Often we find that we can't meet our own standards. Something may be missing, or obstructing the action we wish to take. For example, suppose we characterize ourselves negatively as "old." Really, there's nothing to do in this case; we can't go out and start "being young." Being old isn't an action that we can perform effectively or ineffectively, and being old isn't a failure to measure up to some standard within our reach.

Even so, this perspective may still open something new. What doesn't fit is that "being old" appears to have nothing to do with action. So we can ask ourselves to take another look at our negative characterization. We may find that behind the assessment of "being old," we're dissatisfied with ourselves in some domains of action, and we account for this by saying that we're "old."

It may be that we don't go out often enough with other people; we don't consider or take new directions in our lives (such as going back to school, learning a new hobby); we don't exercise enough or participate in sports. Those are domains of action. Once they're identified, we can take action to shift our assessment.

Given the interpretation of characterization and standards that we explore here, two questions come to mind:

- What standards of effective action can we set for ourselves?
- What actions can we can take to reach them?

The point is that characterizations can prompt us to action. Characterizations don't settle permanent levels of competence. When we're dissatisfied and characterize ourselves negatively, or when we choose to increase our competence in some domain in which we already characterize ourselves positively, we can take action. We can distinguish standards of effective action in a particular domain, and we can set new standards to attain.

CHAPTER 7

Managing Moods

Many people find that they frequently slip into negative, unproductive moods, and, once in these moods, it can be difficult to shift out of them. We suggest that this happens because *most people have an interpretation of mood and emotion that limits their power to observe and change their moods.* Typically, people believe that their moods are produced by the people and events they encounter. So when things are going well, they're in a good mood and can be involved, productive, and so on. But even little setbacks put them in a bad mood, in which they are inaccessible to others, unable to concentrate, and ineffective in their work. People are buffeted between these extremes as circumstances dictate. It seems as if the moods that can offer more stability in their work—such as ambition, challenge, and serenity—are available only during special occasions: a promotion, a vacation, the birth of a child. They have no capacity to cultivate these moods as part of their everyday lives.

In speaking of moods, we're not using the word strictly in its usual sense of "feelings" or "emotions." We refer instead to the ways in which people's past experiences predispose them to certain actions. For example, an employee who's seen many corporate initiatives come and go with little effect is likely to make only the minimum effort when the next announcement comes along.

He may do little more than complain to his peers about how out-of-touch executives are, reinforcing the cynical mood of the whole group. In contrast, a consumer who's received high-quality products and prompt, honest service at a reputable car dealership will probably patronize them again in the future. Her glowing stories of satisfaction will help build the dealership's reputation in the community.

We can interpret moods in terms of assessments that people have about the future. The employee in our example may expect that the new company effort will not improve the company's reputation with customers or his own possibilities for advancement and job security. The customer in our other example may expect that if she returns to her favorite dealership for a new car, she'll receive good value and be treated well. These aren't assessments that either person makes consciously; it's simply obvious to the employee that no new initiative is going to turn the company around, and it just wouldn't occur to the customer to look for a car anywhere else. For this reason, we sometimes refer to a mood as an "automatic assessment."

The unproductive interpretation of moods leads people to focus on the past, to try to blame their bad moods on some recent event. Since we can't undo the past, this offers little leverage in controlling moods. We propose that to begin to manage our moods and build stability, we should focus instead on the future. When we interpret moods as assessments about our future prospects, we are able to take action, because the future hasn't happened yet. We can choose to take responsibility for our moods and to resolve to take actions to improve our prospects.

Another challenge to managing our moods is the fact that we are constantly immersed in the assessments of the people around us. Very soon any group begins to have a mind of its own, something that drives it and gives it a sense of purpose. Any group develops standards for behavior that it expects all members to uphold. We take other people's opinions as indications of our future, as if they were inevitable truths about our personal character, so there is enormous pressure to conform.

By taking moods out of the purely personal, subjective realm and into the realm of assessment, companies can begin to take action to produce and shift moods in their organizations, teams, and customer relationships. We can design practices for helping people to shift out of unproductive moods, for building trust in internal and customer relationships, and for cultivating a mood of satisfaction with customers.

Whatever the source of a person's negative mood may be, he or she can begin to shift out of it by:

· Identifying the assessment
The person may ask himself or herself, "What is the assessment about the future implied by my mood?" (Some typical moods and associated assessments are shown on the following page.)

· Grounding the assessment
The person may inquire, "Is this assessment grounded?" By "grounded" we mean that a person can point to specific observable actions and events—not just the opinions of others—to support their assessment. Here are five questions to ask to prepare a grounded assessment:

What is my **concern** for making this assessment? (What do I want to **accomplish** with this assessment?)

What **domain** of action am I restricting it to?

What **assertions** can I provide to support or refute this assessment?

What **standards** in this domain am I committed to?

What **actions** are now possible?

· Speculating about new assessments and actions
When a person decides that a negative assessment is ungrounded, that in itself often begins to break the mood. In either case, the person may ask himself or herself, "What mood and assessment do I want to build toward?" and "What actions can I take that would create a more positive assessment about my prospects?"

· Resolving to shift out of the mood and take action
The person may declare that a different assessment about the future is possible, and that he or she is committed to take the actions that will bring about that new possibility.

Typical Assessments for Some Negative Moods

Negative Moods	
Resignation	"Nothing is going to improve this situation. It has always been this way and it always will be; there is nothing I can do to change it."
Despair	"There is a disaster approaching quickly; I don't see how anyone can prevent it. I don't know what to do next."

Distrust	"I don't believe that you really intend to fulfill the promise you made to me," or "I don't believe that you are able to fulfill the promise you made to me."
Resentment	"You have limited my future opportunities, and it's useless to complain to you." Also often, "Those jerks have screwed us up again and the people in authority (they) refuse to listen to our complaints."
Confusion	"I don't see what is going on here. I don't know what to do next. I don't see anything good coming out of this situation, and I don't like it."
Panic	"I assess that I'll never be able to keep up with all of my responsibilities if I do not work harder and faster right now."
Arrogance	"I already know what's going on here. Your comments may be interesting in a way, but if you want the real truth about this situation, then listen to me."

Typical Assessments for Some Positive Moods

Positive Moods	
Ambition	"There are future opportunities for me in this situation, and I am committed to take action to make them happen."
Serenity	"I accept that the future is uncertain, that both good and bad will come unexpectedly, and I am grateful to life."
Trust	"I believe that you are sincere and that you are able to fulfill your promises to me."
Acceptance	"I understand that there are certain things that I cannot do and cannot change, but I am still grateful to life."

Wonder	"I don't know what is going on here, but the world seems full of new opportunities, and I like it!"
Resolution	"I see opportunities here and I am going to take action right now."
Confidence	"I have successful experience in this area, and I am competent to act in this situation."

If people do not recognize that moods and assessments can be examined and shifted in this way, negative moods threaten to become permanent lifestyles, as if the future is already settled. Even when they feel good, people are worried about the really bad thing that is going to happen next. People caught in this trap cannot develop serenity or ambition about their future.

Here is where mood begins to be connected with a wider question, beyond any transitory mood or particular situation. For in the long term, a person's mood—whether he or she moves with confidence, eagerness, and ambition—is driven by his or her interpretation of the future in general. A common belief is that the future is basically an extension of what is going on today. From this, and the notion that moods are assessments about future prospects, it is easy to see how people get trapped in negative moods and become ineffective. If something bad happens, it is as if their entire future will be determined by that event. Everything seems hopeless, and they don't see any possibility of taking action to repair the damage.

And so we find that to manage our own moods and cultivate enduring strong morale, we need a different understanding of the future as well. We suggest that the most important key to generating moods of challenge, confidence, and ambition is to understand that people create the future in the commitments they make to each other and the actions that they take together. This notion—that we invent the future together—can be the source of a great sense of serenity.

Our capacity for invention is not limitless. We must learn to accept those things that are clearly impossible: we will not live forever, and we cannot fly without machines to help us. But for most of the events and situations that put us into bad moods, we always have a way out—taking action with others. The future is always unfolding and has not happened yet. It's a future in which a person can make a difference. He or she can be committed to participate in inventing the future. That's the core of a person's identity: people see each other in terms of how they work with others to create future possibilities. And when people really own that commitment, they can build moods of challenge and serenity, and avoid getting caught up in temporary setbacks and the moods of others around them.

Moods and Teams

Learning how to manage moods is also a key responsibility of a productive team member. Since negative moods close off possibilities and disrupt our coordination with others, moods are not just "personal." They are a morale issue and a productivity issue. Managers need to watch the moods of their team and help individuals to manage their moods.

People who fail to manage their moods exhibit a lack of respect for their teammates. Instead of counting on these people to fulfill their role on the team, they constantly have to take up the slack and work around them. In contrast, when we see a particularly effective team at work, the team members seem to be "in tune'" with each other. While they may not think of it in these terms, they are committed to maintaining their team in a mood of ambition, focused on the future that they are inventing together.

Certainly we are not suggesting that people can avoid being affected by, for example, announcements of layoffs. But when people get trapped in a mood, when it becomes their standard attitude about their work, it is really a personal choice. We suggest that whether they think of it explicitly or not, people take one of two fundamental stances: life is something that they are inventing, or life is something that happens to them, and they react to their circumstances.

When people make this second choice, they are doing two things. They are absolving themselves of responsibility, which can seem like an easy course to take. But they are also cutting themselves off from the power to improve their circumstances, and to build their own identity in the world. The widespread presence of moods of cynicism, victimization, and resentment demonstrate the prevalence of this attitude in many of our institutions today. These moods are a major obstacle to teamwork, as well as to building the trust between different functions of an organization that is required for crossfunctional initiatives.

Cynicism is a kind of resignation in which a person has given up on the possibility of change. Cynics are no longer committed to the values and goals of the team or company. Instead they are hanging on for other reasons, such as their position, salary, benefits, and so on. Frequently these people voice complaints like: "The company is so big that I can never move it." Or, "Nobody listens to my suggestions." Or, "They are giving me 'make work' and refuse to recognize my true capabilities."

Victimization is an attitude in which all of a person's moods and circumstances are the fault of others, or of an unresponsive system. These people live in the story that they have no real power in the organization, but they also have no commitment to build power. Everything that happens to them is beyond their control, and they do not see that this is largely a matter of their own choice.

The **resentful** person feels that other people in the organization aren't pulling their weight, but isn't about to say that outside of a small group of friends. He or she separates the company into three groups: his or her own team, which is working hard and getting things done, the "jerks" that are causing all the problems, and the people in authority who refuse to do anything about these jerks ("them"). It's a mood in which a person abdicates all personal commitment by refusing to talk to the "jerks" or "them" about what needs to be improved.

People can declare who they want to be and what role they will play in the company. They can commit to the missions of their teams, and to take action toward fulfilling those missions. They can commit to staying out of these destructive moods, and to being open to talking about them when they arise unnoticed. They can be authentically critical and skeptical where they see the organization needs improvement. This means to speak up and try to change things or honestly work to improve their own part of the whole. Above all, they can commit to avoid swallowing or whispering complaints behind peoples' backs, because that's the road to resentment. They may be greeted with hostility by some for taking a stand, but in the end, if they can prove that their way is valuable, they will get the credit.

Guidelines for Managing Negative Moods

The purpose of this exercise is to enable you to begin to observe the underlying assessments behind a particular mood, and to begin to identify actions you can take that will shift your assessments and hence your mood. As you identify a negative mood in a particular domain of your life, please follow the following guidelines for exploring your mood and the possibility of shifting it.

1. Awareness

Become aware of your sensations (feelings).

2. Choice

Are you ready to make a commitment to alter this mood? If yes, continue to number three; otherwise, by when will you decide, or are you at peace with this situation and do not see a need to alter your mood?

3. Investigation—what or who is this mood about?

What is the narrative you tell yourself while in this mood?
Is it based on an assessment or an assertion?
> If it is an assessment, is it grounded or not?
>> What standards are you using?
>> Are they shared by the people you work with?
> If it is an assertion, is it true or false?
>> If true, what is it going to take for you to accept this?
>> If you realize that it is based on a false assertion, does your realization begin to shift your mood? If not, is your negative mood really about something else?

4. Plan for Action

What's missing?
Which of the moves from the coordination cycle do you need to make (revoke, counteroffer, request, etc.) to bring about what is missing?
Do you need to make a complaint?
Do you need to apologize?

5. Take Action

With whom and by when?

6. Complete

Have new opportunities opened up as the result of completing this exercise? If so, what request or offer could you now make?

CHAPTER 8

On Trust

Managing moods and maintaining mutual commitment to the invention of a shared future is one aspect of productive teamwork. Another critical element is building trust. *Trust is crucial, not only for internal relationships, but for customer relationships as well.* This is because we invent the future in the commitments and promises we make to each other about actions we're going to perform. The members of a team all rely on each other's promises to take actions to fulfill the team's mission. And a transaction between a company and a customer is nothing more than an exchange of promises: the provision of a product or service for appropriate compensation. Because people who accept promises rely on others, trust is always a critical issue. People aren't about to hand over a part of their future to someone they don't trust.

Trust is neither a spontaneous nor an arbitrary feeling. It is not something we develop from "inside" as some ambiguous, personal, internal phenomenon. Trust is built in relationships when we demonstrate real concern about the well-being of others and manage our commitments rigorously. In our interpretation, trust is a mood that involves several related assessments. When we trust someone, we judge that a person is sensitive to our concerns and will fulfill his or her promise.

This is rarely a conscious decision. Generally, we experience this mood as an undifferentiated attitude about a person. We either trust the person to fulfill the promise or not. But we can also distinguish a number of aspects of trust. In doing so, we can learn both to be prudent in making our own assessments of trust and to identify actions that can build trust with others.

First, we don't typically trust people unreservedly in all domains. We might trust a physician to make promises to take care of our body, and not trust him or her to fix our car. We might trust someone to make promises to attend business meetings on time, but not to be punctual at family affairs. Also, we can distinguish three separate concerns that are always relevant to our assessments of trust. (These concerns appear briefly in the accompanying exhibit, Fundamentals of Trust.) Whenever we accept a promise, we make a judgment of the other person's sincerity—whether the person actually intends to do what has been promised. We also assess the person's competence to take the actions promised and his or her involvement—the commitment to the relationship. We can trust people in one of these areas and distrust them in another.

We can distinguish four separate concerns that are always relevant to our assessments of trust in partnerships: **sincerity, competence, reliability, and engagement**. Whenever we accept a promise, we make a judgment of the other person's sincerity—whether or not the person actually intends to do what has been promised. We also assess the person's competence and reliability to take the actions promised and his or her engagement—i.e., commitment to the relationship. We can trust people in one of these areas and distrust them in another.

Fundamentals of Trust

Sincerity: The assessment that a performer is serious in his or her commitments. The performer does not make promises that he or she does not intend to fulfill or that he or she is unable or incompetent to complete.

Competence: The assessment that a performer is capable of performance in some domain. The performer builds this assessment by recurrently performing according to accepted standards.

Reliability: The assessment that a performer is capable of reliable and timely performance. The performer builds this assessment via the recurrent and rigorous management of his or her promises, by either completing promises on time or counteroffering, revoking, or declining in a timely fashion.

Engagement: The assessment that a performer is committed to the future well-being of the customer and the possibilities for collaboration. The performer builds this assessment by listening to the concerns of the customer and continually articulating new conditions of satisfaction for them. The performer also demonstrates respect for the customer as a partner by respecting confidentiality and refraining from alliances with competitors.

Sincerity

When someone makes a promise to us, we open new possibilities and simultaneously expose ourselves to potential problems. One of the risks we take is the possibility that the person may not be sincere. People are sincere when their promises are consistent with their own thoughts or what they say to others. Conversely, we say a person is insincere when we assess that he or she is hiding something—that he or she has a "private conversation" that is different from the spoken commitment.

When we've had past dealings with someone, we've usually developed some general impression of his or her sincerity. But we often face the need to accept or reject a person's sincerity without any prior experience or reports from other people to ground our assessment. Sometimes an opportunity arises suddenly, and if we take time to investigate the person, we'll miss the chance to take advantage of the offer. We also may find that the appearance of questioning a person's sincerity can be damaging to a relationship and isn't worth the risk involved.

In such cases, people often react according to a few predispositions for trust. These are like lifestyles; each person has a characteristic attitude toward new situations. We distinguish four possibilities: trust, prudence, naiveté, and distrust.

The trusting person is aware that people may be insincere, but typically accepts a promise when there is no obvious reason for not doing so. A prudent person will always investigate before making a request or accepting an offer. The naive person trusts unreservedly with no thought to the possibility of harm. And the distrustful person is suspicious and hard to convince, even when there is reason to believe a person's sincerity.

Each of these predispositions contains a certain danger. The naive person will receive the benefit of sincere promises but is also highly likely to be manipulated by others. On the other hand, distrust can restrict both our capacity to coordinate actions with others and new possibilities that may develop. Trusting people are open to new possibilities, but also expose themselves to risk.

One might think that the best course would always be prudence—i.e., not being suspicious but minimizing risk by investigating the sincerity of the person making the promise. In a rapidly changing world, though, life can be like a very fast dance that continually presents us with requests and promises. If we were to take the time to gather evidence for all our assessments of sincerity, we would lose other opportunities. Often, we simply trust or distrust, deciding in favor of either opening new possibilities or avoiding risks.

Competence

When we receive a promise, we need to also assess the person's competence. An assessment of competence refers to the person's ability to perform the actions necessary to fulfill the promise. We could assess that despite his or her sincerity, the person is not competent to deliver the conditions of satisfaction.

Let us take an example. An eight-year-old child says, "Mummy, don't worry. You can go to your meeting. I'll cook the dinner tonight." That mother may positively assess her child's sincerity and, at the same time, she can negatively assess that he has the competence to do what he is promising. There are other situations when we could have a positive assessment of a person's capacity to fulfill a promise, and we could object to her or his sincerity.

What we have said about trust in relation to sincerity can now be seen, with the same distinctions, related to competence. This means that we can speak of trust and distrust as assessments of a person's competence to fulfill a promise. What is important is to acknowledge that sincerity and competence are two different domains and that when we make and receive promises, we assess others and are assessed in both domains.

Trust in Reliability

Reliability is an assessment we make of someone's capacity to manage the distinctions of effective coordination. We say that when someone makes a promise to us, we must also assess not only the competence of a person to deliver the specific conditions of satisfaction involved in that promise, but also the person's general competence in the various moves of coordination required to produce mutual satisfaction. Is he or she able to fulfill the promise on time? When he or she fulfills the promise, is he or she fulfilling what we asked? If he or she is not clear on the conditions of satisfaction, does he or she ask questions to find out? Does he or she call in a timely manner if he or she cannot fulfill the promise, or cancel and make a new promise? These are some of the observations we make and the questions we ask to determine if someone is reliable.

Reliability is a crucial aspect of competence and is especially important in business relationships. Often we think of reliability in terms of recurrence. People are reliable when they can perform some action not just once in a while, but whenever requested.

When we make a promise, we normally anticipate the actions needed to complete the conditions of fulfillment. But we cannot predict the future. We may need to alter our priorities and resolve unexpected problems. In these circumstances, we may need to revoke the promise.

Whenever we do so, we need to consider the consequences. Not managing a promise effectively with a teammate can affect a person's reputation for reliability, and not managing a promise to a customer can sour a relationship, or perhaps even lose an account. The cost of revoking a promise may be even higher. For instance, if someone's promised to chair a meeting, and right before entering she's told that a member of her family has been injured in an accident, she might need to revoke her promise. She may assess that despite the potential cost for her team or company, she must take care of her relative.

Managing promises effectively and revoking them when appropriate builds the mood of trust in our relationships and contributes to our dignity. It is important not to become slaves to our promises, attempting to complete all our commitments despite the cost to ourselves. Furthermore, there are actions that we can take to reduce the cost of breaking a promise and preserve our reputation for reliability. We need to promptly alert the person to whom we made the promise. We could offer an alternative way to address the concern involved in our promise. We might offer compensation for damages we may cause. We may need to explain why we changed our priorities. And, we need to know and accept that whenever we mismanage a promise, we may pay in terms of our own identity, the reputation of our team, and the reputation of our companies.

Engagement

We are concerned with sincerity, competence, and reliability whenever we accept any promise. In some situations, such as making a simple request that can be completed immediately or buying a commodity product, these may be our only concerns with trust. But in a longer-term relationship, such as buying equipment that needs maintenance or contracting for custom-designed products and services, engagement becomes a crucial issue.

Engagement is an assessment we make about the future of a relationship. We say there is a high degree of engagement when individuals or corporations are strongly committed to continuing a relationship, and little engagement when they are committed only to the immediate transaction. Among the members of a team, engagement involves a long-term commitment to the team, to the team's current mission, and to the development of new projects. Companies and their customers are engaged when they have a strategic relationship, perhaps even collaborating on the development of new offers.

Neither high nor low engagement is inherently good or bad. A crack team can come together to handle a single emergency. A company can deliver excellent service on only one occasion. On the other hand, a team can persist by sheer inertia when it is no longer needed. If a company has little competition or the cost of switching between providers is large, customers can become trapped in an unsatisfying relationship. In this case, market conditions, and not superior service, maintain the relationship.

CHAPTER 9

Building And Leading Teams: Producing Conversations For Managing Commitments

Building and leading teams are recognized to be activities essential for effective businesses. The large number of courses, seminars, workshops, and retreats offered to develop these competencies demonstrate how widespread the concern with teams is. Despite the popularity of the leadership industry, a real competence in building and leading teams is uncommon, and there isn't a generally accepted way to teach these competencies. Many people in leadership roles are resigned to never becoming leaders of an effective team.

The lack of competence in building and leading teams and lack of agreement about how to arrive at competence comes from a shortcoming in our common-sense understanding of teams. Common sense tells us that a team is a group of individuals interacting to achieve particular objectives. Our main issue with this understanding is that it does not allow us to gain competence in building and leading effective teams because it fails to take into account how teams are effectively constituted and maintained. *Here, we propose an understanding of leadership as the ability to build teams through cultivating the right conversations at the right times.* In all effective teams, sooner or later, leadership shows up. This happens because leadership is demanded by the necessity to coordinate action in a coherent way. Leadership is be present when the team is constituted and will play an active role in its constitution. When this is not the case, if leadership doesn't appear quickly, the team disintegrates. In this way, leadership is a human phenomenon that cannot be separated from the phenomenon of team.

This chapter makes two central claims:

- Leadership is a phenomenon of the conversations of a team, not of an individual. In these conversations, the leader takes action to ensure that the conversations of the team take place and that these conversations are assessed by the team to be effective. The leader is the person who's granted authority by the team to take care of these conversations in an ongoing manner;
- A team participates in a set of ongoing conversations among people who commit to share an explicitly declared mission and to coordinate actions to fulfill the mission.

Team Conversations and Commitments

It simply isn't enough to assemble individuals side by side and call them a "team." No group, such as a group of experts, constitutes a team unless they're having the conversations that we call the conversations of team.

In our research, we've found that the following conversations are constitutive of teams. In other words, teams cannot remain teams and succeed in the projects they undertake unless people in the team have ongoing and effective conversations regarding the following nine commitments.

1. A commitment to coordinating action for the sake of a shared, explicitly declared mission.

Team members commit to take care of what's been declared to be missing. In other words, all team members commit to "play the same game" and to ensure that the "game" continues to be played.

To share an explicitly declared mission and to coordinate action to fulfill it is a radically different understanding of team than a team as a group of individuals side by side pursuing some common unarticulated or implicit purpose. The possibility of a team is called forth by the declaration of a mission. It is this explicit declaration that brings people together once they commit to share it in action.

We can illustrate our point with an example. Even people who work in the same department, see each other every day, and make requests and promises of each other every day may have different assessments of what the mission of their team is. We would assess, in this case, that the mission is *not* shared. Moreover, even if people in the same department, when interviewed independently, use the same words to say what the department is about, they may not be sharing the mission. *This is because the shared mission shows up in the assessment that each team member makes about the actions performed by the others on his team.* The mission may become rearticulated a number of times until it resonates with the assessments of all members of the team. Only when the actions taken by the other teammates are consistent with his or her understanding of the mission will a team member assess that the mission is shared.

In order to ensure that the mission is shared, the leader requests each member's public commitment to the team's mission. In recurrent review and staff meetings, leaders make assessments of the team's performance in fulfilling the mission. The leader makes explicit how the sharing or the lack of sharing of the mission, as it shows in the teammates' actions, is contributing to or jeopardizing the team's performance. The leader also produces the appropriate conversations that assure that his or her individual assessment about the team's sharing of the mission is an assessment shared by everyone else on the team.

2. A commitment to own the shared mission.

The team members are committed to fulfill the mission by means of taking all legitimate actions that will contribute to the mission's success. To own the mission is to evoke the assessment that actions will be taken recurrently to fulfill the team's declared mission. Excuses aren't justifications for failing to fulfill the mission and aren't offered to team members nor accepted from team members in this mood. There are continual conversations for action—making requests, offers, promises, etc.—so the team's mission is fulfilled again and again. Most important, to own the mission is to make and speak assessments of concerns, breakdowns, and opportunities for the team to fulfill the mission.

By taking action in this way, an identity is produced in which both dignity and self-esteem are at stake in fulfilling and having fulfilled the team's mission. Lack of ownership shows up as negligence, lack of passion, and resignation.

3. A commitment to fulfill roles by each team member, with explicit accountabilities.

To fulfill the mission, the team's work is divided into domains. Each member of the team has a particular identity or role, depending on the domain he or she commits to take care of. More precisely, inside the team, each member has assumed responsibility for the successful contribution of a particular domain toward fulfilling the team's mission.

This doesn't mean that a team member will act only in his or her domain, however. "Being responsible" for a domain doesn't mean that each person takes action only in that domain or that the person responsible for the domain is the only one able to take care of that domain. A person assuming responsibility will make sure that:

- actions are taken in this domain in order to fulfill the team's mission;
- the actions taken in other domains are consistent with the actions being taken in this domain;
- the actions being taken in this domain are also consistent with the actions being taken in other domains.

Traditionally management has referred to this as "division of labor." More than a **division of labor**, this is a **division of responsibilities** within an understanding that ultimately everybody on the team is accountable for the success of the overall mission of the team.

The role of the leader is a key identity on the team. As we've already pointed out, the leader's role is to be the team leader, and, as such, his or her domain of responsibility is to make sure that all the conversations of the team take place effectively.

Often breakdowns are related not to a lack of competence or lack of ownership, but because the identities aren't clear to everybody in the team. In sports, for example, a team may lose the ball because no one moves to catch the pass in the designated spot on the field. The leader makes clear initial declarations of roles and clarifies them or modifies them whenever interpretations diverge from the initial identity that was declared for each team member.

4. A commitment to develop and carry on practices for anticipation.

The leader and each teammate commit to anticipate future breakdowns as well as future opportunities to accomplish the team's mission. We include here the practices of planning, establishing periodic milestones for assessing accomplishments, declaring breakdowns, speculating, formulating action, making tentative suggestions, and opening new conversations for action (requesting, offering, etc.). Additionally, we include here practices for reconstituting the team's unity when breakdowns produce miscoordination. (Weekly review meetings might help prevent that.) Also, we include the practices for learning and innovating new competences, individually and as a team. We refer to the latter as "training," especially in sports. The leader is always assessing the team's and each teammate's competencies and declaring with them new domains of learning. The leader's concern for learning isn't restricted to individual team members; leaders are also concerned with new "games" that the whole team could play to fulfill the mission according to new standards not previously available.

5. Commitment to the team's unity of command and to the political declarations of the team.

"Politics" are the conversations that determine what conversations a community has, when these conversations will take place, who the speakers and observers will be, and who will be excluded. As we've proposed before, the leader's role as the team leader is to make sure that the conversations of the team take place. Unless the leader has been granted the authority to play this role, however, sooner or later these conversations will fail to take place and the team will face the danger of disintegration.

Note that people on a successful team commit to the leader's being the team's political authority, and grant him or her the authority to execute his or her declarations. (We refer to commitment to the role of leader; people commit to the person in this position.) As part of this commitment, people on the team commit to respect and to put in practice the leader's declarations of mission, division of labor, and standards. (This doesn't mean that the leader is a tyrant, of course. On the contrary, tyrants sooner or later find themselves isolated and abandoned by a team.)

Making declarations is just one part of the leader's job as team leader. The leader is also responsible for engaging the team in conversations of design. In these conversations, each teammate brings his or her competences and concerns to play in inventing new possibilities. After these conversations, the leader makes declarations.

6. A commitment to evoke and produce trust.

Teammates commit to be sincere, to act on the basis of grounded competence (including producing the assessment that they're reliable in the way they manage their commitments), and to be engaged in a future relationship with their teammates. At the same time, they commit to have public conversations when they have negative assessments about other teammates' sincerity, competence, and engagement.

The leader ensures that each teammate's commitments are managed rigorously. When people are incompetent or unreliable, the leader takes action to redefine the roles in the team and/or to provide coaching. When the leader reaches a grounded assessment of insincerity about somebody on the team, he or she asks for an apology and for repair of the damage produced to the team's identity. (And repeated insincerity should result in separating that person from the team. This isn't a moral assessment. An insincere person poses a problem for the team because he or she can't be counted on to share the team's mission in action.)

7. A commitment to a mood for success in the mission.

Teammates commit to elicit and design a mood consistent with success in fulfilling the mission. Key moods for a powerful team are ambition, acceptance, serenity, respect, membership, pride, camaraderie, and celebration. Of course, this doesn't mean that "negative" moods—moods that close future possibilities—will never be triggered. Negative moods can happen to anybody, including the leader. The commitment here is to observe resignation, resentment, anger, arrogance, and so on, as moods—as automatic assessments rather than as "reality"—and to intervene to shift the negative assessment of possibilities. These interventions are effective because, first, they announce the mood that's observed, and then they act as an invitation to produce a new mood or to deal with the concern of the current mood. Finally, the intervention invites speculations and new conversations for action to shift the mood. This commitment also includes designing—anticipating and producing—what will evoke the moods the team needs to succeed.

The leader is the guardian of the team's mood. (As a matter of fact, this is a domain where a leader can't afford to be less than competent!) Leaders may address the mood of the team in scheduled meetings but also won't hesitate to address moods at any time that they might jeopardize teammates' commitments. Where the leader assesses himself as not having the competence needed to intervene or to design a new mood, the leader won't hesitate to request help from someone with proven competence.

8. A commitment to the team's standards for assessment.

Here we include commitment to the standards for assessing the team's performance both in the domain of team and in the specific projects being undertaken. Distinguishing the domains of conversations of the team isn't enough. Each team has to declare specific standards for assessing performance and learning in these domains, and the teammates need to commit to share the same standards. A similar commitment is required when declaring the operational mission of specific projects. For example, standards for completion need to be declared and the teammates commit to share these standards.

In their conversations for design, the leader invites all teammates to participate in building the team's standards. Again, when the leader reaches resolution, he makes a declaration and asks for the public commitment of each teammate to these standards. After the declaration is made, only the leader has authority to change the standards (and when this happens, a new public declaration is made).

Of course, any team member may request the adoption of new standards, but they may only be adopted with the leader's endorsement.

9. A commitment to the future of the company, the team, and the people's careers.

A successful team has each teammate's commitment beyond the completion date for a particular project. Teams don't survive when members behave like mercenaries (in this case, maintaining commitment only to the particular task and its completion date). In successful teams, participants fuse their personal identity with the team's identity and develop a concern for the team's future viability.

Taking care of the future viability of the team transcends the practices of planning and training we've already referred to. It entails taking care of the future viability of the company, making alliances inside and outside the company to ensure the team's viability, and last (but not least!), taking care of each teammate's career. An effective leader will make sure that conversations are happening that align the future of the company with the future of each team member.

Team Leadership

In the long run, to be the team leader, it's not enough to make the declaration of mission upon which the team was founded. The leader develops in her commitment to the mission and in her competence to keep people engaged in the team's conversations. Leadership will become apparent when people grant the leader the authority to lead the team toward succeeding in the mission.

A leader's authority is granted by the institution the leader participates in and by the community being led. Invested with the authority of a leader, the leader's role is to design conversations and practices so that the team conversations are taken care of. The leader isn't presumed to be "best" at doing all the team's work, nor to be competent in all domains, nor to always have all the answers and immediate solutions to all breakdowns. To fulfill her mission, the leader consults with people inside and outside the team and delegates actions to other teammates as necessary and appropriate.

An effective leader doesn't need to be "perfect." In a team that's assessed in its public identity as having an excellent leader, the leader isn't necessarily a virtuoso and a master in each and every one of the team's domains. *To excel as a leader is to put together and to orchestrate a team that has strong competencies to be successful.* To excel as a leader is also to be competent in building alliances and bringing in help where competence is lacking. A team that relies exclusively on the leader's virtuosity or mastery is, in the long run, a weak team. It will not grow and produce other strong leaders in their domains of responsibility.

In summary, the leader as leader has to have the boldness to ask for and to hold the final authority on the team for declaring the mission, for assessing performance, and for requesting commitments from team members. The leader must be clear that his role is to declare what's satisfactory for the team and its mission. *Fundamentally, the agreement of leader and team must be that the team members satisfy the leader in the performance of their duties.* If it happens that the team is assessing whether or not the leader is satisfying them, the structure of the team is disempowered—the leader is not a leader and the team is in jeopardy. The leader brings forth partnership on the team concerning the team's mission, not consensus, and takes final responsibility for assessing the teammates' actions and declaring completion. In the end, it is important to keep in mind that leadership and the ability to build teams are not qualities and capabilities you are born with, but rather, they are domains for learning and skills that you can acquire in time.

PART 3

The Other Side of Speaking

CHAPTER 10

Understanding Concerns
Behind Requests

When we make requests of others, we do so in order to satisfy the concerns that we have. Even when we ask others for specific things, it's because those particular things are our best current interpretation about how to take care of our concerns. We can only ask for what we know about, based on our own unique history and experiences. So focusing on a customer's needs is only one way to satisfy his or her concerns, and perhaps not even the best way. Being sensitive to the customer's concerns, rather than the stated need, opens up a larger horizon of possible actions that would satisfy the customer. The sensitive listener brings more value by bringing his or her own interpretation of concerns and the actions that can best satisfy them. When we get the sense that someone is attuned to us in this way, we have more trust that he or she understands our situation, and more confidence in his or her ability to take action on our behalf.

When we speak about the concerns that motivate our actions, we are not speaking simply of needs, desires, or wants. Needs and desires are usually for specific things, like my need for a pen or my desire to own a Ferrari. But usually, and especially in complex situations, we don't walk around with a clear

87

interpretation of what we want other people to do for us. For example, a top executive tells a department manager that she must develop better relations with the local community. The executive's request to the manager doesn't contain a specific thing or task the manager must do. The executive does not, for instance, ask the manager to hold special events, sponsor local schools, or donate to local charities, though it might be necessary to do some of these things. Nor would it be of any use for the manager to ask the executive precisely what he means. He probably doesn't have anything specific in mind, and besides, it's very tiring to be constantly telling people exactly what needs to be done. Rather, in this example, what the executive did was express a concern, inside of which the manager is free to invent.

What is a "concern?" We commonly speak of our concerns as things that are important or matter to us, or things that occupy our attention—that with which we are "concerned." It's not wrong, of course, to speak of such things as "concerns," but they are concerns in a sense derivative of the concept of concern that is relevant to our consideration in this essay. A thing is only important, it only matters to us or engages our solicitude, because of some purpose or desire or belief we hold. We have a concern for money because we need to buy food or pay rent or want to take a vacation. It is this structure of concern—the way in which some purpose or end we have in mind organizes our activities and the objects we employ—that we need to explore.

So concerns in the sense relevant to this essay are those basic ends upon which all of our purposive actions bottom out. The concerns we are interested in are thus, in a manner of speaking, teleological; they are the human goals that make intelligible our practices and employment of objects. Such basic concerns always operate within a concrete domain. That is to say, they always organize an actually existing network of objects and a set of practices into some more or less coherent whole.

We will have considerably more to say about this later, but one can easily imagine several illustrative examples. For instance, obtaining nourishment is a basic human concern. In the United States, this concern organizes several practices (grocery shopping, eating out at restaurants, ordering out for pizza, waiting on tables, farming, canning, television advertising, FDA inspections, etc.) and the objects involved in these practices (such as stores, cars, shopping lists, packaging) with their distinctive technologies (electric stoves, homogenizing, refrigerating). Because activities and objects within this domain occur against the background of this concern structure, we immediately and without reflection understand most of the activities we ourselves and others in our culture engage in. If my neighbor goes into her backyard and lights some charcoal on fire, I immediately understand her action against the background of the concern structure of securing sustenance. If my neighbor instead goes into her backyard, digs a pit, and covers it with leafy branches, I would probably not understand her to be attempting to procure food (I might not find her activity intelligible at all). At the same time, we can imagine cultures in which setting traps are a central practice in the "food" domain of concern.

This last example demonstrates three other important features about the structure of concerns. The first is that concerns are, for the most part, "transparent." The second is that a concern is constituted by, and constitutive of, its domain. The third is that the domain of concerns encompasses practices and objects that differ in respect to their centrality or marginality to the concern in issue.

To say that a concern is transparent is to say that concerns usually operate in the background. In other words, most of the time we engage in practices and employ objects, and understand why others are engaging in practices and employing certain objects, without any explicit thoughts about the concern that is motivating them. Moreover, concerns only operate within a cultural context or style that both opens up and at the same time limits possibilities for action in general.

By focusing on concerns as they operate within a cultural context or style, we are attempting to illuminate that part of the overall structure of the cultural context or style that makes purposive action intelligible. Concerns, as we've seen already, require an understanding of the possible uses of equipment and practices within a given cultural context or style. But to make activities and objects fully intelligible, we need in addition to this understanding to know why someone is acting and employing objects in the way that she is. In a certain sense, I can understand my neighbor's activity on its own: she is digging a pit, and using a shovel in the way that one appropriately uses shovels within the cultural context or style we share, but I don't understand her unless I know why she is digging. Concerns provide the basis for this latter kind of intelligibility.

It is only in "breakdown" situations—situations that don't readily fit into any of our given domains of concern—that we consciously try to discern the motivating concern. This may seem counterintuitive given certain connotations of the word "concern": isn't a concern precisely the kind of thing that is present to the mind? Before being able to adequately answer this question, we need to consider the assumptions that make it plausible.

There is a view of human action and intentionality that draws a distinction between the inner and outer. Such conception concerns, understood more generally within the realm of beliefs and desires, are inner, mental states to be sharply distinguished from the physical objects and bodily motions that are observable, and that occur in the outer, physical realm. Such a picture of the relationship between mind and world has largely dominated thinking about human action for the last several centuries. The view we advance, by contrast, challenges the intelligibility of this distinction. Concerns on this view are not subjective experiences manifested in behavior. Denying this, however, doesn't commit us to denying the reality of concerns. Concerns are real, but they are entirely constituted by the relationships they establish between practices and objects. In other words, once we see the structure concerns impose on practices and objects, we know all there is to know about what concerns are. There is no need to discover what mental experiences the concerned subject might have, or what mental states she might be in.

That this is how concerns are generally experienced can be illustrated by paying attention to the way concerns usually work in our lives. Most of the time, we purposely act and interact with people and things without any thought for the concern that is motivating the action and on the basis of which the action is intelligible. In the course of our daily routines, no deliberation is usually necessary to decide what to do or how to do it in pursuit of our concerns. For instance, I experience no process of rational deliberation in deciding that I need to make a shopping list; I don't first consider my deepest and most general concerns (concerns for nourishment or health), derive from those the need to obtain food, and reason from that need concerning the best alternatives for action (making the list, driving to the store, withdrawing money from an ATM, etc.). Instead, most of the time I skillfully and unreflectively perform the everyday activities essential to the pursuit of my basic concerns. Something like a mental experience of a concern only appears when an object or activity resists incorporation into the pattern of purposive intelligibility that concerns normally provide. We call these occasions that resist incorporation into the structure of concern "breakdown" situations.

Activities and objects must manifest some structure of concern on pain of being considered irrational or unintelligible. A breakdown situation within my neighborhood and culture could be my neighbor digging a pit in her backyard. If I can discern no concern motivating that action, I will likely think that my neighbor has gone crazy. Several concerns might offer themselves: she's digging a pit so that she can plant a tree in order to beautify her yard, and thus she's concerned with aesthetics; or, she's digging a pit to install a swimming pool, and she's concerned with recreation. Other less likely concerns might offer themselves: she's digging a pit to trap an animal, and her concern is food; or, she's digging a well to obtain water, and her concern is nourishment or cleanliness. These concerns would be unlikely to provide the appropriate background for understanding her activities, however, because animal traps and backyard wells are no longer part of the dominant network of objects and technologies for satisfying those concerns.

This brings us to the second point, the constitutive nature of the domain of concerns. A domain of concern is nothing other than the set of objects and practices that are organized within it into some intelligible pattern. As such, the domain of concern defines the objects and practices involved as the objects and practices that they are. Objects and practices are holistic. In other words, objects and practices are defined by the place they hold within a whole network of other objects and practices. A shovel is what it is only in virtue of its **relation** to other objects and equipment—dirt, wheelbarrows, sod—and its typical employment in certain practices—digging, mixing concrete, etc. Of course, the fact that a shovel is typically related to certain objects and practices doesn't mean that a shovel couldn't come to be employed in other contexts. A shovel could be used to apply paint to canvas, but if such applications ever became commonplace, it would mark a change in what it is to be a shovel (as well as what it is to create a work of art).

What all this highlights is that there are never concerns in the abstract. Returning now to our previous discussion about the relation between mental and physical, or inside and outside, we can see more clearly why concerns are not "mental" phenomena. On the view we reject, all that we would want to know about concerns is what's in the head of the concerned individual—what is her concern. If we had direct access to this knowledge, we wouldn't need to observe her behavior; we would already know all there is to know about her concerns. On the view advanced here, it makes no sense to think about concerns existing independently of the world. All that there is to a concern is the structure that it gives to practices and objects.

As a result, when we make claims about the permanence of concerns, or concerns shared across cultural and temporal boundaries, what we are referring to is either a large degree of overlap between the objects and practices that constitute the domains of concern in question, or agreement in the practices central to that domain. For example, what all domains of concern for nourishment share is the central practice of eating and drinking. They might differ in all other particulars: the actual foods eaten, the practices for eating (chopsticks or forks or fingers), the kinds of food eaten, or the other concerns with which eating is linked. But the presence of this central practice allows us to equate our domain of concern with very different domains in other cultures.

At this point, we might consider a possible objection to the view being advanced. Aren't some concerns just facts of human existence, needs imposed, for instance, by the biological makeup of the human organism? Eating seems a good case in point. We're not concerned with eating because of some historical accident of culture; we're concerned with eating because we must eat to stay alive. This observation is valid so far as it goes. Of course there are certain facts imposed by nature, and natural constraints that cannot be exceeded without penalty. But one interesting feature of the concern structure as we now see it is that the most important thing about such biological needs is the way they are interpreted and woven into our other practices and concerns. For instance, in some cultures eating is linked not just with concern for nourishment, but with religious concerns. Strict dietary codes are followed and enforced, and eating takes on a spiritual dimension. Biological demands for nourishment, in such a configuration of concerns, might be subsumed to religious concerns, as evidenced in practices of fasting and asceticism in general. In other cultures, the concern for nourishment is linked to a broader concern for health. One could imagine other configurations of concerns linked to eating; eating might be linked primarily to the concern for entertainment. Practices such as regurgitation might then be employed to overcome biological constraints on the pursuit of this concern. Indeed, one unique feature of human existence is precisely the way our concerns allow us to reduce the demands of nature to near insignificance, and we can all imagine instances when choosing death would be intelligible given the background concerns of the individual and culture in question.

Turning now to the third point mentioned above, we need to establish one more distinction in order to complete our analysis. This is the distinction between practices and objects central to a concern, and those marginal to the concern. Every concern will, at any given time, have a fairly well-defined structure of relations between objects and practices, generally accepted as being the normal way one pursues that concern. At the same time, there will be a variety of objects and practices that also gain intelligibility in terms of the concern structure, but are only marginally relevant to that domain. The best illustrations of this, because they are so prevalent, are observed in historical shifts in the concern structure. At one time in Europe, for instance, the practices central to the concern for societal order revolved around the central practice of monarchy. Other, more democratic practices existed in limited realms or regions, or were at least preserved conceptually in literature and theory, but were only practiced within the margins, so to speak, of society. Now, of course, the situation is reversed; democratic practices are central to Western concerns for governance while monarchic practices are marginalized to the point of near extinction. Another example is provided in the practices central to the concern for gaining an education or learning a profession. At one time, a central practice in that domain involved training through apprenticeship. Until fairly recently, legal training, for example, was achieved almost exclusively through apprenticeship. With the establishment of the Harvard Law School in the beginning of the nineteenth century, a marginal practice for receiving training as a lawyer was established in the United States. Through the closing decades of the last century and the beginning decades of this century, legal training through universities established itself as a practice central to that domain. Now, a law degree from a certified law school is a prerequisite to being licensed as an attorney in many states, although apprenticeship remains a marginal practice for obtaining a legal education in a few jurisdictions such as California.

It is also important to note that basic concerns themselves can be marginal or central in the overall background understanding that shapes an individual or a culture. Spirituality, for instance, is a basic concern that has largely been marginalized in Western technological culture. Different cultures and historical epochs will consequently offer different sets of concerns as possible domains for activity. Because concerns are principally not subjective experiences, but rather the purposive structure of the world, we can speak of domains of concerns as public and shared.

Now that we have set out in rather general terms the structure of domains of basic concerns, we are ready to see how we can use concerns as a distinction to help us see and understand the practices with which we are most closely involved. Practices, as we have seen, gain their intelligibility against the backdrop of a concern structure. At the same time, implicit in our discussion has been the recognition that through changes in culture, technology, and other broader societal features, the concern structure can also change. Certain marginal practices can gain prominence within the domain, other central practices can be marginalized, and in a variety of ways new practices can be assimilated to the concern structure. This can happen, for example, through technological innovation, or through a creative reconfiguration of concerns. Because of the holistic nature of practices, this will also result in changes in the practices themselves.

This change might happen at the level of unities or practices. Or, it might happen more globally at the level of concerns themselves. The former type of change occurs when a new unity or practice is introduced to a domain of concern, or an existing unity or practice becomes incorporated into a sphere of concern different than the one with which it is currently involved. We can see in the continuing advance of technology the way introduction of new networks of equipment affects entire domains of concern. One need only consider the impact that radio, movie, and television technology had on the domain of recreation. The practices created by these technological advances have, in turn, been partially displaced by the introduction of VCRs into common use. The impact on the practices once central to recreation has been enormous and has reconfigured entire industries devoted to satisfaction of this concern.

An example of change resulting from the coupling of new concerns with practices (rather than objects) is provided by the interjection of the legal profession into corporate transactions. At some point, businessmen recognized the value of lawyerly skills (careful and technical interpretation of documents and preparation for litigation). The result has been a reconfiguration of the practice of being a lawyer, with an explosion of transactional and contractual work to the point where a sizable portion of the legal profession spends little or no time in a courtroom pursuing traditional lawyerly activities. There has been a corresponding change in the domains of concern of business organizations, which are increasingly sensitive to the potential legal consequences of financial decisions. The objects involved in business transactions also have seen a corresponding change—agreements that at one time were set forth in a few pages are now exhaustively detailed in contracts comprising several volumes.

A more global change occurs when the relationships between concerns as a whole shift. Returning to an example alluded to earlier, a concern with food that's linked to a concern with spirituality might come to be dissociated from religious practice and become linked instead to concerns for health. As a result, eating and cooking practices would naturally shift to reflect the latest scientific learning regarding health. New, subsidiary concerns over cholesterol and low-fat eating, calories, nutritional value, bran, etc., would be introduced. These would spawn a variety of new practices and alter many others. Activities once unintelligible (like willingly eating bran muffins) would become common.

In this essay, we have identified four important features of concerns:

(1) Concerns are the purposive structures that organize and coordinate practices in intelligible ways;
(2) Concerns operate for the most part transparently, and we ordinarily notice them only in breakdown situations;
(3) Concerns are constitutive of the practices they render intelligible; and
(4) Concerns themselves can be either central or marginal to an identity or cultural context or style, and they make the practices that they organize central or marginal.

Being sensitive to these features of concerns will allow us to antici-pate changes in the constitution of practices with which we are concerned. Understanding features one and two makes it possible to question the activities with which we are most intimately concerned to illuminate the concern struc-ture within which we work. Seeing the ground of our purposive actions in this way will make us sensitive to feature three and help us anticipate ways in which unities and practices might come to be reconstituted as our basic concerns are reconfigured. One important way this occurs is suggested by the centrality or marginality of practices to our concerns, or shifts in the centrality or marginality of concerns to our identities, are an important source of change and innovation. Another important impetus for reconstitution of concerns, practices, is derived from the cross-appropriation of objects and practices from one domain of con-cern to another.

CHAPTER 11

Recurrent Domains Of Human Concerns

In this essay, we set out to distinguish the structure of concerns that's constitutive of every human being's life. By "constitutive" here, we mean the structure of concerns that make up the substance of human actions, possibilities, and assessments. We set out on this project in order to make ourselves observers of these constitutive concerns. Typically, we claim, all of us are in these concerns without observing them as recurrent structures of life. Then we're not typically able to produce for ourselves conversations to design ourselves—our actions, possibilities, and assessments—in these domains. We lack the linguistic distinctions necessary for such a conversation. Our purpose in this essay, then, is to provide those distinctions and enable such conversations for design.

"Domains" are the domains of recurrent concerns of human life—concerns that we cannot escape as human beings. All human beings have breakdowns in these domains, act in them, characterize themselves and other people in them, and look ahead to and invent possibilities for themselves in these domains. Examples include education, career, sociability, work, self-worth, and aesthetics or play. We'll give fuller treatment to what these domains are as we go along.

We said that these are recurrent domains of human concern. We leave open the question whether they're the domains of concern for any human existence, in any place, and in any time; that question is open to speculation. It may be that we'll be able to understand classical Greek civilization, the civilization of ancient China, the civilization of the tribal Aborigines of Australia, and any other human life or civilization in terms of this same set of permanent domains of concern. What would make each "civilization" or "society" or "culture" distinct would be the "discourses" in which they live in these domains — the histories of institutions, practices, and understandings unique to them. What we claim with confidence in this essay is that, ***within Western civilization, these are recurrent, unavoidable domains of human concern***.

Every person lives in a set of conversations to deal with these domains of concern. He or she has an understanding of what education is, of what people need to be educated in, of what constitutes the worth or dignity of a person, of what's available to a person as a career or a direction to take in life. This understanding shows up in what expectations we have of ourselves and of others, by which standards we judge ourselves and others. The career or direction in life that a middle-class urban American in the twentieth century can take is different from the career or direction a peasant farmer of Nicaragua can take, or even from the career or direction an American of the nineteenth century could take. Ultimately, what's different isn't the opportunities that the world objectively holds out for him—it's the discourse he is, the historical conversations in which career possibilities have been articulated for Nicaraguan farmers or twentieth-century Americans. These historical conversations "possess" him; he isn't in control of them. They allow him to see the possibilities that he sees—for example, to continue the tradition of farming or perhaps to join a Nicaraguan guerilla military group, or, for the American, to become an engineer or a doctor. And they close him to possibilities that he cannot see—for example, for the American to become a farmer or guerilla fighter or for the Nicaraguan to become an engineer or doctor. ***It's not his own choices or the limitations of his objective situation in the world that open and close his possibilities; it's the "discourses" that he is, that he as an American or a Nicaraguan and his "society" or "culture" have inherited.***

None of the claims we've made so far should be clear to you as a reader yet; we've set a direction here for your thinking as you continue to read. We're going to be laying out the domains of concern as linguistic distinctions throughout the rest of this chapter. What we've done so far is offer only a glimpse of the whole thing so that you can see where we're going.

Before going on, we need to say something about what kind of activity an investigation like we're doing here is and who we are to be doing it. No one is privy to the final truth or understanding about anything. Every investigator speaks in his own time, with the foundations and limits given by his own concerns and the concerns of his time. Every observer and interpreter observes and interprets within the language that he speaks, the concerns that he is, and the possibilities that he sees. *No observer is the observer of what is purely and simply given by reality; all observations and all interpretations are the observations and interpretations of persons grounded in and limited by the historical time in which they observe and interpret.*

These limitations are our limitations, too, as we write essay. We write as investigators at a particular time, limited by the stage our investigations have reached and by the particular concerns we are at the time in which we live.

But these historical conditions that limit us also make our investigation possible. It is because our investigation has reached the stage that it's reached, with our understanding of language, breakdowns, action, and characterization, that we can say what we say here about domains of human concerns. And it is because we live in the time that we live, with our concern for education and the design of the self, that we can construct and design an interpretation of the self in terms of permanent domains of concern. None of what we say here finishes any aspect of the theory of education or the self—what we do here is what is possible for investigators and designers in their particular historical setting.

Domains of Concerns

Domains of concerns are distinctions that we, as investigators, invent for observing the concerns that human beings are. And we believe that it's possible to produce a list of the domains of concerns that every human being is. We base our list on our understanding of human beings as linguistic beings, with the capacity to speak and listen—that is, to create distinctions in the world in language and to act in the world made intelligible to them in linguistic distinctions. In other words, human beings are the kind of creatures who can create a language of distinctions for objects, such as chairs, rocks, clouds, and apples; for actions, such as running, lifting, sitting; and for assessments, such as good, tall, wide, and intelligent; and who can act together in that language—sitting in chairs, requesting apples, and so on.

Our list is divided into three groups, in accordance with three distinctions we make about human beings.

1. First, human beings are linguistic beings and, as we'll show, live in concerns unavoidable for linguistic beings.
2. Second, human beings live in history: they're historical beings, born into a world of conversations already going on, with practices and institutions already established. And we'll distinguish domains of concern unavoidable for such historical beings.
3. Third, human beings are selves: they have permanent identities over time. And we'll claim domains of concern unavoidable to beings with such identities to care for.

Those three—linguistic beings, historical beings, and selves—aren't separate in human life. Every human being lives in language, history, and identities simultaneously. Our history is linguistic. Our identities are linguistic. Our history is a history of identities. Our identities are historical. We're all of these beings at once. The distinctions we make here are for the sake of analysis, for making rigorous observation possible.

Human Beings as Linguistic Beings

The first group of domains of concerns that we're going to distinguish has to do with the conditions of our existence as linguistic being—the concerns that we cannot avoid having because we're beings who participate in language.

We'll distinguish each domain of concerns in a separate paragraph—five in all for this discussion of human beings as linguistic beings.

> *Our BODIES—their health, their availability—are an unavoidable domain of concern for us as human beings.* Language is ultimately a biological phenomenon. Speaking and listening can't happen except as biological phenomena in the bodies of speakers and listeners. The possibility of participating in conversations and of completing actions formulated in conversations depends upon our bodies. To participate in conversations, we must make ourselves present, bodily, whether face to face with another, on the telephone, writing on a piece

of paper, typing into a computer, or something else requiring our bodily presence.

The world we produce in linguistic distinctions allows us to act. Once we've distinguished and practiced such actions as sitting, walking, boiling an egg, writing a letter, driving a car, and such, they become automatic. We don't think about them anymore; we don't anguish over them, plan them, worry about them, or otherwise think about them as we perform them. They become "play" to us. Such actions include the actions we perform while at play, without attaching any great significance to them or often to their outcomes. Perhaps most of the time, we're creatures that "play" or "dance" in such automatic actions. To be in "play" in this way is one of our concerns to be able to escape self-conscious, intentional activity for comfortable, often purposeless activity. In this essay, we call this domain of concerns "play" or "aesthetics." We use the latter term, "aesthetics," to evoke the activities of art, such as painting, dancing, and sculpting, without some narrow usefulness for the activity.

Language is social. It's the social creation of distinctions for acting in a world together. In order to participate in language, we must participate in conversations with other people. In other words, we need to build for ourselves networks of people with whom we participate in conversations. In this chapter, we call this permanent domain of concern "sociability."

We ask others to talk with us, we open conversations with others, and we assess ourselves and others in this domain (for example, as "friendly," "unfriendly," "secretive," "open," and so on). Included in this domain are concerns for not only meeting and beginning to talk with people, but also for establishing trust as the possibility of speaking and listening openly with people. In order to act together in a coordinated or cooperative manner with others, we rely on them to "mean what they say;" that is, to make promises they'll keep, to make assertions that they believe to be true themselves, to produce distinctions they continue to act consistently with, and to make requests they're serious about seeing fulfilled. We realize that there will be exceptions; that, sometimes, others will lie to us, deceive us, or in some other way betray our trust in them. This issue of trust—our concern that we can accept what others say, that they're not hiding a private conversation that conflicts with what they say to us—is part of the domain of concerns we're calling "sociability."

When we say that these are permanent domains of concern for human beings, we aren't saying that all human beings are constantly, consciously concerned, for example, about establishing networks of trustworthy people for conversations. Most of the time, all of us live without explicitly considering such matters. *Most of the time, sociability (and the other domains we're talking about in this) is in the "background."* We're not explicitly aware of them, but at any moment they may become conscious concerns for us, in breakdowns. For example, when our trust is betrayed or when we lack people for conversations we consider important, sociability becomes an important, explicit concern. We may then openly assess the trustworthiness of the people around us or question who we would open new conversations with, to secure ourselves from similar breakdowns in the future. The same is true of the other domains of concern we're identifying here. Our bodies don't become explicit concerns in our everyday conversations until a breakdown occurs—for example, we become ill, or we can't attend a meeting because we must be somewhere else. *The domains of concern we're identifying here are the permanent structures of the breakdowns and explicit concerns that appear in day-to-day life.* They show up in our fears, our celebrations, and in our assessments and characterizations of ourselves and others. They're the structure of concerns that cannot be avoided in human existence.

Every human being is born into a *family*. The family is a natural network of conversations. It provides a domain of concerns that aren't a matter of the individual person's own interests. The family is a network of shared concerns. For example, the health of other family members is a concern for each of us.

In cooperating and coordinating our actions in language with other persons, we make promises to them. We say that we'll complete some action by a certain time. Making the promise doesn't complete the action. Then, insofar as we act to fulfill the commitments we make in language to perform actions, we're concerned with *work*. We're concerned to fulfill our own commitments to act, and we're concerned that others around us fulfill commitments to act that they've made to us. In our day-to-day lives, this domain appears in our concerns that a job get finished, in our planning how to complete work on some project, and in our character-izations of ourselves and others as "diligent," "lazy," and so on—whether they're effective in completing the actions they've promised to perform.

Those five domains—*body, aesthetics or play, sociability, family, and work*—are the domains we claim to be conditions for linguistic existence. In other words, they're domains of concern for human beings as linguistic beings. They're drawn from what is necessary for speaking and listening—a body in which speaking and listening are generated as biological phenomena, "play" in action in a world made intelligible in linguistic distinctions, a social network of speakers and listeners, the sharing of concerns with others, and work to fulfill commitments to act made in language.

Human Beings as Historical Beings

The next group of domains, which includes education, career, money, and "the world," has to do with concerns we cannot avoid as human beings, insofar as we are historical beings. Human beings are born into a world of conversations already going on. In those conversations, standard practices have already been invented; then, as human beings, we're born into a world of others already participating in those standard practices, with expectations, anticipations, routines, etc., that we don't yet participate in.

The world around us embodies a history that we need to catch up with. And, as human beings, we have futures. Our futures aren't determined for us; we have to invent them in the conversations we have. Our history, including the history of the world around us, provides a basis for the futures that we invent. Our futures are the continuations that we invent of our history of conversations.

The first recurring domain of concern we distinguish in this group, based on the historical existence that human beings live, is *education*. This domain is that of concerns for becoming competent in the standard practices of your world. Developing competence in these practices is necessary to your viability in the public world. You need to perform competently in some practices in order

103

to make your living—some skill, trade, or profession. And competence in such standard practices and everyday skills, such as reading and writing, driving a car, or reading a map, and skills of social participation, such as speaking, manners, and social ethics, are necessary to your social viability—your acceptance in conversations with others. Concern for gaining competence in all of these skills falls into what we're calling the domain of education, or learning.

Every human being has before him the question of what he's going to do with his life. In part, this is a practical concern for making a living. **But it's more fundamentally the concern for inventing a direction for the possibilities and actions of your life.** We're calling this domain of concerns the domain of *career*. This domain is that of concern for what future you're going to invent for yourself—what standard practices you're going to develop competence in, what areas of public breakdowns you're going to deal with, what new possibilities in what standard practices you're going to invent.

No human being can avoid concern for his biological and social viability. Each of us tries to secure the conditions of life—food, shelter, clothing—to ensure his future. And each of us tries to secure others' trust for his future conversations—for example, to be able to exchange promises with others and to be trusted in the marketplace. In our own time, such concerns may appear as the concern for maintaining good "credit"—assuring that others will be willing to offer something to us now in return for our own promise to provide something to them at a later time. We call this domain of concern *money* or *prudence*. It is the domain of concern each of us has for his future viability in the public world. Money itself—cash, investments—is a tool for securing that viability.

Every human being lives in a community of others, with whom he participates in organizations and institutions. This community may be a political community, with laws and institutions of government. It may be a professional community. Or it may be a less formal community, like a circle of friends, with informal institutions and practices, such as weekly card games or lunch meetings. *Membership* in such communities is the domain of concerns we're distinguishing. Membership provides the possibility for participation in the institutions of a community. For most of us, our political membership in a state provides us with the possibilities of participation in a system of money, a system of civil and criminal laws, organization for actions on a scale not possible for us as individuals (scientific research, for example), and more.

The history of the world around us is larger than what bears on our individual lives. There are other "cultures," "peoples," "societies," or "civilizations" than the one we live in. And our concerns are larger than the breakdowns and issues of everyday life. We're concerned about the future of our country and the future of our world, beyond the scope of our own lives. We're concerned about the welfare of people we'll never meet in places or times we'll never visit. We're concerned about finding out more and more about our world and the universe it lies in. In this essay, we call this domain of concerns *the world*.

Human Beings as Selves

The final three domains of concern we're going to distinguish here arise from the existence of human beings as "selves," with individual perspectives on the world for observation and assessment. These three domains are *dignity, situation, and spirituality*.

1. *Dignity*

Every human being is concerned that his actions and possibilities be valued and are in the interests of his own integrity—that he act consistently with his own declarations of standards for action. This domain of concern for assessing oneself is what we call *dignity* here. "Valuable" is an assessment that one makes, in the light of public understanding of what is valuable. The public understands that actions and possibilities toward alleviating poverty are valuable, for instance. Every individual sees himself measured against such an understanding and assesses himself. We should emphasize that it isn't a matter of "fact" whether an individual's actions and possibilities are valuable—public standards don't decide what assessment he makes. It's perfectly possible, for example, that Albert Schweitzer could assess his actions in medicine in Africa as pointless, despite public opinion, and it's also perfectly possible that someone of little repute or admiration, even among those close to him, could value his own actions as extremely valuable. "Integrity" is also an assessment that one makes about the consistency of a person's actions with his own declarations of the standards or virtues he'll live by. If you've declared for yourself that you'll live a generous life, say, and you never contribute to charitable causes or volunteer to provide help to others when you could do so, you may assess yourself as lacking integrity. In that case, you're saying that you don't live by the standards of action you set for yourself.

2. *Situation*

Also, every human being makes assessments of and is concerned about the possibility of doing something positive in the world and in life, given the situations they find themselves in. This unavoidable human concern is what we're calling *situation* here. In other words, everyone is concerned to assess the events that have taken place around them, their competences and limitations, and the competences and limitations of other people with respect to the negative and positive possibilities they hold for themselves. "Positive" and "negative," remember, are assessments that each of us makes, and any one person's "situation" only exists in that person's observing what he calls his "situation." Thus, a person who observes events, himself, and other people and assesses himself to have only negative possibilities—he suspects his wife will ask for a divorce, that he won't be able to keep up his house payments, etc.—will be depressed. We say he's in a depressed mood. A person who observes his situation and assesses himself to have many very positive possibilities—he has a new job that he expects will present new challenges and rewards, his children are doing very well in school, etc.—may be optimistic or enthusiastic. These terms for moods— "depressed," "optimistic," "enthusiastic," and others—are what an observer says about the person. They're terms an observer uses to characterize a person in this domain of concern. The person himself may not explicitly assess his own situation—more typically, he falls into a mood that others observe and then attribute to him assessments of his own possibilities. We say, for example, that he is depressed and sees no possibilities for himself, or that he's elated and sees many new positive possibilities.

3. *Spirituality*

Finally, **each of us is an observer of the facticity of life**. No one can avoid observing that, in some respects, life is the way it is, regardless of what you wish or regret, and regardless of what illusions or hopes you may live with. We're all here, we'll all die, and life has unavoidable structures, like the structure of concerns we've distinguished here. This unalterable character of life is what we call the "facticity" of life. Nothing anybody says or does changes the facticity of life. A concern for

106

the facticity of life is not a narrowly practical concern. It's not a concern for feeding yourself, providing for your family, ensuring your future viability, or anything similar. Nevertheless, it's a concern that we cannot avoid insofar as we are observers of the facticity. We accept it, perhaps in accepting that we will die or that the future isn't predictable. Or perhaps we wonder at it, say, in celebrating our own life despite its concerns. Or perhaps we refuse to accept it and build illusions to take its place, say, that we can defeat death or control everything that will happen in the future. We ignore the facticity of life if we ignore the fact that we will die and act as if we had infinite time in our lives to pursue every possibility. We call this concern for the facticity of life *spirituality*.

These are the thirteen domains we propose as unavoidable, recurrent domains of concern for human beings. These aren't the only domains of concern you may distinguish for some purposes—for example, you may want to distinguish such domains as business, farming, or banking, depending on your purposes, on what you want to call attention to in observing people and actions, proposing actions, or making characterizations of people. What we're saying is that these thirteen that we've distinguished here are unavoidable and recurring domains for observing and designing our lives.

Domains, Breakdowns, and Actions

We've said that these thirteen domains are unavoidable domains of concern for every human being, regardless of the time or place in which he lives. They are also domains in which familiar, day-to-day concerns and breakdowns arise. To help you better understand how these domains appear in everyday life, look at the following chart of the thirteen domains and familiar concerns and breakdowns within them.

Thirteen Recurrent Domains of Human Concerns: Possible Breakdowns

1. *BODY*: health, sickness, injury, availability and unavailability for meetings and appointments.

2. *PLAY* or *AESTHETICS*: entertainment, recreation, art, and appreciation of art.

3. *SOCIABILITY*: opening new conversations, making new friends, maintaining friendships, breaking friendships, trusting what others say, establishing trust for yourself.

4. *FAMILY*: having children, education of children, marriage.

5. *WORK*: completing actions you have committed to take, doing your job.

6. *EDUCATION*: gaining competence, skill in some area.

7. *CAREER*: choosing a direction to take in life, choosing a career or profession to prepare for and follow.

8. *MONEY* or *PRUDENCE*: having sufficient money to support yourself, your salary, reputation among others you deal with.

9. *MEMBERSHIP*: participation in club, professional, organizational, or government institutions; gaining membership in societies, clubs, or other organizations; becoming a citizen.

10. *WORLD*: politics, the environment, other countries or cultures.

11. *DIGNITY*: self-respect, self-esteem, lack of self-esteem, conflicts between your standards of action and your actions.

12. *SITUATION*: disposition, temperament, outlook, emotions, judgments about "how things are going."

13. *SPIRITUALITY*: philosophy, poetry, religion, humor (laughing about our nonacceptance of the facticity of life, not being burdened by it).

FAMILIAR CONCERNS AND BREAKDOWNS

Not everyone lives with all or even some of these particular breakdowns or familiar concerns. We give the list only to illustrate how our thirteen permanent domains of concerns allow us to observe everyday breakdowns and concerns.

We're saying that all of these thirteen domains of concern are unavoidable in everyone's life. That claim is a claim about the facticity of life for our linguistic, historical selves. We, and every human being, live in these domains. No one can escape them.

Our claim is not, we emphasize, a claim about the "truth" regarding human existence. Our claim is a claim for the design of ourselves as observers of our own lives. Other designs might be proposed, and the one we propose here may be modified. What is important is not knowing the final story about human existence; what *is* important is how we construct ourselves now as observers and designers of our own lives. And what we propose is that we observe ourselves as participants in these thirteen domains as unavoidable, permanent domains of concern—that we observe our actions, our possibilities, our breakdowns, our assessments and characterizations, all within the structure of these thirteen domains.

We've looked already at familiar breakdowns in the thirteen domains. Now let's look at another chart, this time showing common types of actions and possibilities for action in each domain.

Thirteen Recurrent Domains of Human Concerns: Common Types of Possibilities For Action

1. *BODY:* exercise, medical checkups, traveling to an appointment.

2. *PLAY* or *AESTHETICS:* taking a vacation, going to the movies, going to an art museum, painting, putting a puzzle together.

3. *SOCIABILITY:* inviting a new person into a conversation, meeting an old friend, declaring a person trustworthy or untrustworthy.

4. *FAMILY:* getting married, sending children to college.

5. *WORK:* finishing a report, writing a letter.

6. *EDUCATION:* enrolling in a class, reading a book.

7. *CAREER:* choosing a major in college, getting a new job.

8. *MONEY* or *PRUDENCE:* investing money, bargaining for a new salary, buying health insurance.

9. **MEMBERSHIP:** joining a professional organization, becoming a citizen of a new country, founding a new club.

10. **WORLD:** working in a political campaign, visiting another country or culture.

11. **DIGNITY:** declaring pride in your work, declaring that your work is significant or insignificant, declaring standards of action for yourself to live up to.

12. **SITUATION:** declaring that your future is good or not good, declaring that you have more possibilities than you have been seeing, declaring that you have fewer possibilities in life than you supposed, discussing your possibilities with other persons.

13. **SPIRITUALITY:** reflecting on the facticity of life, going to church, philosophical discussions with others.

These are examples of the kinds of actions all of us perform, given that we live in those thirteen domains of concerns. Our actions and possibilities in life aren't random; they have the structure of the concerns that we are—we act on the concerns that we live in. For example, within our concerns for ourselves as bodies, we go to the doctor for medical checkups, we travel (we move our bodies) to be present for actions we've committed to perform, and so on. Within our concerns for our families, we consider schools to send our children to, we care for our children, wives, husbands, and parents, and so on.

A point we should note here is that *the types of actions and possibilities we listed in the chart need not each fit into only one domain*. For example, "reading a book" is a type of action that could be taken in what we've called the domain of education, but it could also simultaneously be an action you take out of concern for your career, your family, or your body. As observers of our actions and possibilities, in the midst of different concerns at the time we observe, we will say that the same action or the same possibility will be generated out of different concerns. For example, say that you've just returned from a vacation in California. If, as an observer, you're in the midst of concerns for play, you may observe your action (taking a vacation) as generated out of your concern for rest and recreation. If, as an observer, you're in the midst of concerns for sociability, we may observe your action as generated out of your concern to meet new people or renew old friendships. The thirteen domains aren't always separate in life—they intersect and appear simultaneously in everyday breakdowns and actions.

We won't enter here into an extended discussion of the structure of domains of actions and possibilities that we participate in. What we want to do here is only to show how the domains of concerns we've distinguished show up in our day-to-day actions and possibilities. It's important at this point only to see that the types of actions we formulate, take, and observe are types of actions within the domains of concerns that we are. Typically, most of us regard actions as movements of our bodies, and our possibilities for action as generated by the possibilities for movement our bodies give us. What we're saying now is something very different: *our possibilities for taking and observing action are generated by the structure of concerns that we are*.

CHAPTER 12

On Listening

We have been discussing at length all the various skills that require having structured conversations. There is another set of skills required for having conversations that build commitment and allow people to build the future together; namely, skills for listening. The following chapter is an introduction to the concept of listening itself, describing distinctions that will allow the reader to begin to think about listening in a new way. It is not intended to be a guide on building effective listening skills as this topic requires a collection of essays of it's own.

This chapter seeks to explain what must be done for listening to occur in an effective and significant sense. To do this, first, an account will be given of how listening is generally understood, even by those who practice active or engaged listening skills. Secondly, the requirements for the success and the necessary ultimate failure of this understanding will be explored. Thirdly, a new model of listening will be elaborated.

Current accounts of listening take for granted an information-processing model of the mind and a designative (or instrumental) view of language, even when expressive aspects are taken into account. We will show that the mind doesn't normally function like an information processor, and language isn't primarily instrumental.

A genuine understanding of listening ought to depend upon how people act when things are going along smoothly. A new paradigm of *disclosive* listening will then be developed in which listeners attend to the dimension in which speaking takes place in their customer's company and become attuned to that.

The Current State of Listening

Nearly everyone concedes now that listening to another person is a difficult skill to master. It requires more than just hearing and understanding the words enunciated; it also requires figuring out what the other person assumes and therefore leaves unsaid. That is, it demands a sense of the other person's perspective and concerns. Additionally, effective listening requires an attentiveness to the expressive side of a person's language: the facial expressions he or she makes, the gestures, the tone of the speech, all of the things that we tend to call the person's "body language." And finally, listening requires the hearer to be able to inhabit the speaker's perspective. Without these skills, listening becomes a matter of just recording; it's not responsive, and *listening in its strongest, best sense must always be guided by the endeavor to respond to the speaker*.

Businesses recognize all of this when they note that their sales representatives fail to understand the concerns of senior executives, think strictly in terms of technical problems, fail to build rapport, fail to note what customers have left unsaid, or fail to ask the sorts of questions that draw out the genuine meaning of the customer's statements. But the solutions proposed over the years to correct these failings, while well intentioned, ended up contributing to the problem. This is a fairly large claim, so we'll have to look at it in parts. First, what are the solutions that are commonly attempted? We'll start by examining the way companies train sales representatives to deal with senior executives, and we'll elaborate on four aspects of this training.

When senior executives create visions about how to make their company achieve profitability and competitiveness, companies seek to train their sales representatives to draw out the senior executive's vision and then to determine how the sales rep's company can help him in achieving that vision or in forming others.

When sales representatives fail to note what the executive isn't saying or fail to pick up on the expressiveness of his utterances, companies train their sales representatives in active listening skills.

One way is by training sales reps to check their understanding by paraphrasing what the executive has said in the sales rep's own terms. In this way, the sales rep draws the executive into an educational process. A similar solution is provided for sales representatives who don't know how to respond to expressive cues: they're taught to ask if the executive is annoyed or weary or whatever the sales rep assesses the expressive content of the executive's behavior indicates, and then those particular sentiments are handled directly and reasonably.

When companies think sales representatives are too technical and aren't providing enough solutions, then they're instructed to learn as many facts as possible about the executive's industry, the executive's company, and where the customer's business is having breakdowns that the sales rep's company can solve. In short, the sales representative is trained to become a consultant for a particular industry.

Finally, when all else fails, sales representatives are trained to conduct individual interviews with executive and management personnel at the target company, organize focus groups of those in the client company that use the sale rep's company's products, and finally to survey widely to find out what's going right and what's going wrong.

What could be wrong with any of this? Wouldn't such training produce sales reps who could listen to senior executives and become a true value-added resource that senior executive would rely upon? Wouldn't such training truly provide someone who could listen?

First intuitions are pretty good at answering these questions, even if they don't give us grounds for further thought. What do our first intuitions tell us? Yes, it would be wonderful if each sales rep could have not only a technical knowledge of his home company's products but also knew his customer's field inside and out, and in addition was expert at setting up dialogues where executives developed clear understandings of what they wanted their companies to do. But do companies typically breed such superhuman sales representatives? And if a company somehow managed to produce such wonders, would the client company trust them fully? If it did trust them fully, wouldn't it want to hire them?

For all the skepticism—some might say defeatism—in their tone, these questions are telling. They point out the size and difficulty of teaching people the basic skill of listening. Common sense says that breeding such superhuman sales representatives would be impossible. But common sense also says that sales representatives *do* sell products and some sales representatives are, in fact, valuable resources for the companies that they sell to. What's going on?

Two critical assumptions make training in listening seem a superhuman task. First, behind the four basic aspects of training just listed, it's assumed that people are essentially information processors—that we're basically data-processing minds hooked up to data-sensing organs. So to train a sales representative to listen to senior executives more effectively, the sales rep needs to be shown data similar to a senior executive's and given some of the basic skills for processing that data—in other words, to teach the sales rep some of what the senior executive knows. That way, the sales representative ought to have the right perspective or context in which to evaluate (or process) the senior executive's words.

The problem with this training model is that it's assumed that the sales rep can be taught the senior executive's skills, even though he's not often around a senior executive. Only if we believe that skills are ultimately composed of many rules could we think that we could teach a sales rep, in a classroom, to make the kinds of judgments a senior executive makes. Notice, however, few of us think that we can teach people to drive in the classroom. We normally reserve the classroom for simply teaching people which kinds of phenomena they'll have to pay close attention to while driving: children playing in school yards, the distance of the car up ahead, the blind spot that you have to turn your head to see, the gas gauge, drinking habits, etc. The true skills of driving—actually learning how to maneuver a car— we expect people to learn from being in many situations behind the wheel. We expect them to get a feel for the activity not by being taught many rules but by actually experiencing many situations, so that in comparing one situation with another, the driver can respond to, say, a slick driving surface according to his or her abilities and the car's abilities without any analytical thinking, by just relying on experience. Skills by their nature, then, are situational. Those who think that all that's done skillfully could be decomposed into rules despair of ever truly succeeding at it because the task seems too Herculean, precisely in the way teaching a sales rep to think like a senior executive seems superhuman. Imagine having to learn rules (and rules for applying these rules) that will cover every situation in driving. (Indeed, behind the notion of rules for applying the first level rules lies an infinite regress that even philosophers in the cognitivist and artificial intelligence communities recognize.)

What about getting the sales rep to have a broad knowledge of the client company's industry? The same reasoning applies here. If that knowledge is basically a situation-based know-how, then classroom teaching won't succeed in passing it along to the sales rep. If the know-how at bottom could somehow be decomposed in a way that allows for its transmission in a classroom—not something we believe—that would present an incredibly Herculean task, the same as teaching someone to drive entirely in a classroom.

But this is only half the problem with teaching sales reps to think like senior executives. A company might be content to have sales reps know as much about thinking like a senior executive as a student fresh out of drivers' education knows about driving. After all, the student fresh out of drivers' education can ask questions more attuned to being a driver than the student who's just learned in great detail how the new transmission works and what it can do. So what's the second thing wrong with the four ways of producing better listeners?

The second problem is really an offshoot of the first. The information-processing model of the mind suggests that people really do have deep down in them clear reasons for doing what they do and thinking what they think. If this is the case, then what people do when they communicate is transmit data and ways of handling it. Language, then, turns out to be something that designates various bits of data and ways of handling it. We can see that this view makes sense of training a sales rep to put questions to senior executives in terms of their visions of their company's means of staying competitive, their visions of increasing profitability, and their visions of how they go about coming up with visions. All of these things, the information-processing model of the mind suggests ought to be clear or, in principle, susceptible of being made clear in the mind of the senior executive. So then active listening of the sales rep becomes a matter of the sales rep getting the senior executive to put his vision and his means of forming a vision in the right designative words. And by "right designative words," we mean words that bridge the perspective of the senior executive and the sales rep and his company. For once the sales rep truly understands the data and the forms in which the senior executive wants them in order either to form a vision or to know how well his vision is determining the company's activity, then the sales rep ought to be able to determine precisely the product the client company needs to either enhance or satisfy the senior executive's basic needs.

The active listening skills, the surveys, interviews, focus groups, all of these assume that senior executives, managers, and other product users do have clear visions or can be made to have clear visions—through engaged questioning—about how their jobs are done and ought to be done in the future. And all this assumes that their know-how can somehow be stated in terms of rules or rules of thumb and that it's not based on years of experience about what works in which situation, where what counts as a specific situation has no rigorous definition because the situation is always changing, as is the cluster of relevant similar situations.

Teaching a sales rep to pay attention to his customer's expressive gestures may seem a way out of thinking in terms of information processing and the infinite task it inspires. Because when the sales rep asks his customer to explain the incredulity that the sales rep's remarks about the product seem to have inspired, the sales rep is acknowledging that something other than pure designation is going on when speech is going on. It would seem he's acknowledging that all speaking takes place with a particular passionate coloration, even if that passionate coloration is the gray, drab, but burning, scientific passion of seeking the truth. It seems by talking about the passion of the hour, the sales rep is trying to bring about an agreement in tone. He's trying to get a connection between himself and the client, get some agreement on the coloration of the meeting, to finally get rid of a mood where the client sees everything, no matter what, as impossible or annoying or untrustworthy. To put this strictly in terms of active listening, the sales rep is trying to stop the client from acting out and put him in some form of receptive mood. **But all these approaches assume that an emotion is on the inside of the other person and that language can be used to get clear about that emotion**. Moreover, getting clear about the emotion is also a way of getting clear of the emotion and returning to some space of gray, drab designation. So designation runs through even this attempt to acknowledge the expressive side of language. When clients fidget, roll their eyes, lean back in their chairs, and such, they're designating emotions as much as if they were speaking about them. But designating emotions by using these more active signs gets in the way of the purer designative language, which must be used to get control of less sophisticated, brute, active signs.

Well, what's precisely wrong with this belief that emotions are inside us and show themselves to others in expressive signs? This is certainly how we normally think of emotions. And it's a tremendously useful formulation—it allows us to tell people that they have the responsibility of keeping their emotions under control. We've also all experienced anger, sorrow, irritability, and they don't seem to be features of the world, but rather of us. So, again, what's wrong with this formulation?

The first thing to notice is that we only notice emotions as within us when we've broken off from one or another engaged activity. While we're active in building a spreadsheet or doing our taxes or counseling someone, we seldom notice that we have any emotion. It comes as a surprise to us when our spouse tells us that we're acting grouchy or seem tired. Almost universally, we respond

118

in an irritable way, "No, I'm not." But what's being said here? Just because we're not conscious of our particular mood or approach to things doesn't mean that we don't have a particular mood or approach. And sometimes we *are* faintly aware of a particular mood while involved in an activity. But now the question has shifted. Who is it exactly that has the mood? Is it the deep reflective person or is it the activity that the person is making happen?

Let's approach this insight from another direction for a moment. We've all been to parties that had a nasty mood or feeling attached to them. And we find that most of the time, we're just taken over by this nasty mood. One person says something nasty to someone else, and in that context, nothing else seems possible but a nasty response. If we've settled into the party before this happens, it can't be resisted. The nastiness leaves only if some new strong personality, someone who's not already been affected, enters the scene with a different mood, or maybe the mood simply runs its course. Now are we to imagine that all the people invited to the party arrived in a nasty mood? Or are we to believe that moods are contagious like viruses, but they're even worse than viruses because fewer people are immune to them?

The first of these explanations runs against our common experience. The second seems to cry out for a physical explanation when there is none in sight, no viruses that cause moods in the way others cause colds. Rather, it makes more sense to say that the activity of the particular party—the mix of people, the layout of the food and drink, negotiations with the setting, the conversation started first, the music, all of these—opens up particular possibilities for action in the same way sitting in a Ferrari opens up certain possibilities for action that are different from those of sitting in a Volkswagen Beetle. And these possibilities will only show up clearly in terms of certain moods and emotions that the possibility attracts. The possibility of driving fast in the Ferrari will only show up if the other activities of our life allow us to feel exhilaration. If our child has just died in a car crash and the only car in town that we can rent is a Ferrari, the possibility of all that speed will be a constant irritation or a waste to us in our mourning. The point here of the party and the Ferrari is that *moods aren't so much in us as evoked by the possibilities of our situations.* But the situations aren't personal, for the most part. They're shared in the activities we share with others. This should fit with our common intuition that we only feel moods and emotions that others in our culture feel and recognize. We don't go around claiming to feel something that no one else in the history of our culture has felt before (though if we're poets, we may claim to feel something that others are feeling but we're the first to articulate). Nor can we feel all the same anger and outrages to honor that members of other cultures feel.

Haven't we drifted far afield from language and listening, though? Actually, we haven't drifted at all, because **the most important thing that needs to be made clear about language is that it is not primarily designative—it isn't around to point out things and concepts and rules and ideas—but that it is primarily expressive.** But "expressive" is a tricky term, and this understanding of language runs against our normal everyday intuitions, though it fits with some of our deepest. What's meant by "expressive" here is not that language starts out as and remains grounded in the poetic cry of some inner feeling. There's no eighteenth-century claim here that language is first song and that therefore a senior executive's words should be taken as so much poetic expression of his feelings about his company. Rather what is meant by "expressive" in this context is that language first and foremost functions to draw people into a shared *disclosive space* of a particular kind. This is a dense expression that must be unpacked. To see what's meant here, let's attend to everyday occasions of language use where the designative content couldn't be important.

Suppose two men are sitting facing each other in a sweltering railroad car while traveling through Calcutta. Each is sweating profusely and obviously uncomfortable in the heat, so each knows that the other is uncomfortably broiling away, and moreover, each knows that the other knows about his situation. Nevertheless, it doesn't strain credulity at all if one says to the other, "It sure is hot in here."

On a designative (or instrumental) theory of language, nothing significant has happened; no new information has been exchanged. The words were wholly gratuitous. But we know right away that something important has happened. As soon as the one man completes his sentence, the whole situation has changed. Instead of two men alone eyeing each other, the ice has been broken, and now they're sharing their condition together. Now they're both overheated in a way they weren't before. Now the heat focuses a relationship between them. If the example isn't clear as it is, imagine that instead of two men in the train car, we have a young unmarried man and woman. As soon as one says that it sure is hot, they're together sharing a space for possible disclosure that didn't exist before.

A disclosive space, then, is a space of possibilities. When the two people speak to each other about the heat, a space of possibilities opens up. The important thing to notice about conversations is that they're largely controlled by certain aspects of the particular space of possibilities that opens them. The conversation to follow in the train car will be directed by the mood or style of light and pleasant understatement. To see that this is likely to be the case, imagine that the first says to the second, "We'll both be dehydrated and sick by the end of this trip." The deep chords to which the following conversation will chime will be those of sourness. But to see this phenomenon in a richer way, let's return to the party mentioned a short while ago. Moreover, let's suppose that the first two men who arrive start talking about their investment strategies for the coming year. Suppose too that they agree on little. One sees the economy moving steadily along; the other sees various political decisions causing a disaster. One concentrates more on looking at the value measures of companies and the other focuses on broader, macroeconomic data. Unless they're experienced at handling such situations, the competitiveness of investing in our society is likely to come out in a contentiousness that could turn antagonistic. As more people arrive, they'll be drawn into various modes of responding to the antagonism. Peacemakers, cheerleaders, water carriers, and other such roles will be solicited. And, by and large, the solicitation will be irresistible.

How does this happen? Surely, it's not because anyone chose to perform any one or another of those roles—playing one or another role is done unconsciously. No doubt, habit will have something to do with it; people generally take up roles that they're familiar with. But the mix of people could easily cause someone to take up a role that he or she is unfamiliar with. Well, then, *how precisely do people come to take part in the way they do? They do it by listening.* But they don't listen so much to the particular point of the words of the conversation but to its *style*. They respond to the possibilities opened up by the antagonism. Their listening draws them to respond as richly as possible to the possibilities opened up by the antagonistic style of the discourse. In this way, each person who arrives at the party becomes a participant in its ongoing style. And in doing this, the conversation about the merits of one method of investing over another turns out to drive the atmosphere of the party, which, in turn, may drive what the two men say to each other though, at a certain point, they may wish, out of good will, that the whole thing just stop.

Listening, then, in the first instance and in the above example, *is a matter of attuning oneself to the style of speaking and activity that's going on*. One doesn't first figure out what the words designate and then figure out the style in which they're spoken. Instead, as with the exaggerated expressive gesture and the smile of recognition, the style is primary.

For the most part, people aren't misunderstood because they're describing experiences, ideas, or situations so unusual and so complicated that much more detail is needed for a listener to figure out precisely what's being said. And when there's some sort of technical misunderstanding of what a word or statement refers to, we ask questions. People are only afraid to ask questions when they feel out of tune with the situation altogether. When we say Wall Streeters don't hear what the CEO from the Midwest or Southwest is saying, we don't mean that Wall Streeters don't understand the meanings of the words, but that they're not in tune with the sense of things the Midwest CEO has, with the expressive space he lives in.

But the party and train car examples show us that we ought to mean more than this when we speak of misunderstanding. The misunderstanding doesn't happen because the Wall Streeters aren't attuned to the particular expressive space of the Midwestern CEO, but because they don't establish an expressive space in which they both make sense of each other.

Now we're in a position to see what's going wrong with the attempts to teach sales representatives listening skills. In trying to teach sales representatives the rudiments of senior-executive thinking; or the rudiments of his or her client's industry; or to paraphrase in their own words; or to conduct interviews, surveys, and the rest, the sales representative is being taught to do no more than embody failed listening. *Because the point of listening is not for the listener to come to see things as the speaker does.* This assumption is the mistake of the information-processing theory of mind and the designative or instrumental view of language. (The same information is to be transmitted from one mind to another.)

How many senior managers would be satisfied with discovering that the sales representative from a supplier company is a junior-league version of herself? *The point of listening is to develop a shared disclosive space, to develop a new relationship, in which each has a role that may be developed, not one role in which one member is an expert and the other is an amateur eager to become the master.* The sales representative who spends his time learning about his home company's products, and then about the client industry and the rudiments of the senior-executive thinking in that industry will more than likely find himself with two bodies of knowledge, like accounting and chemistry. He won't have been taught how to form a shared disclosive space between them. If this employee then proceeds to try to bridge the gap with active listening skills or engaged listening or surveys and the rest, he'll find himself developing only one body of knowledge, or developing both but developing them separately. The result will be that he only finds a few more slender threads of connection between the two each time.

For all of these reasons, the current attempts to improve listening are likely to be disastrous, so listening will have to be examined further in order to develop some paradigm examples and to bring out its central structuring principle.

Listening's Structuring Principles

The account of listening given so far needs more substance. However, so far this argument has claimed that the whole information-processing view of the mind along with its designative, instrumental view of language is wrong because people don't primarily listen to words or sentences for their designative content and people don't really try to understand precisely what the meaning of a word or a sentence is as the speaker meant it, given his or her world of concerns and commitments.

The first point goes against designative or instrumental language in rather obvious ways, and the second goes against the information-processing view of the mind because that view suggests that proper communication is a matter of the transmission of the same, identical meanings (data) from one processor to another. There's something fairly radical and counterintuitive in both of these claims. But we've tried to show some clear cases where the designative content of words and sentences isn't at issue and how the expressive content takes control. We've also tried to show one clear case—the party—where new arrivals don't speak for the purpose of imparting this or that designative idea, but for the sake of including themselves within the ongoing activity in the way that best makes sense to them and in a way that perpetuates the activity. Finally, we argued that like the people at the party, sales reps ought to be interested in developing a particular disclosive space in which both their home company and the client company can share, instead of having the sales rep try to become an expert in both companies. To see how this works for the sales rep, we'll have to develop further the insight about listening and speaking for the sake of developing a new space of possible roles.

To see more closely what happens in listening, let's go back to the railroad car case and elaborate on it a little more. We imagine two men sitting in the sweltering car in Calcutta and the first says, "It sure is hot in here." Now what follows is each telling the other stories of how he's had to deal with the heat before: various close calls with dehydration, sunstroke, and the rest are recounted. In the course of this conversation, each gets some idea of what the other is doing in India and what their two competences as men-about-the-world are. But what's happening here? Is some sort of merger taking place between the two men? Is information and the way of processing it that each man had individually now shared? Or are they both engaged in the shared activity of keeping their minds off the heat?

Each of their particular stories builds up a single story in which they both have roles as particular kinds of storytellers. In this case, the fact that one of the two men is, let's say, on some sort of adventure (running away from life in the West and all it entails) and that the other is, again let's say, a relief worker paid by the United Nations—these different vocations mean that the two men probably understand heat prostration in very different terms and engage in slightly different practices in dealing with it. One thinks of it and engages with it in terms of adventures—he stresses his body and mind as much as he can, keeping only the narrowest margin of safety—while the other deals with heat prostration as something deadly to be avoided, because he's seen too many die on its account. Neither needs merge with the other's way of dealing with heat prostration in order to find sense in the other's accounts of it. In fact, as they speak, they'll each find that they did not and do not have fixed ways of dealing with heat prostration that were tied to their fixed occupations, but that they're taking on new roles and altered identities in terms of the development of the shape and style of the expressive disclosive space they're opening up. As one tells a story, he'll find himself coming up with details that he'd formerly passed over as either invisible or as insignificant, but that now make sense in terms of the style of their dealings. So the UN worker might recall looking back on this occasion in this disclosive space that he'd been rather heroic when he tramped down a steep ravine to save the life of a straggler whose own family had given the man up for dead in the heat. They'd both nearly died coming back. Before this act had always shown up in terms of reuniting families, and, in recounting it, he'd dwelled on descriptions of the wife's cries of joy and the children's hugs and all the rest directed at their given-up-for-dead head of the family. But now details of slippery footholds might dominate.

This is not to say that the relief worker simply gets caught up in the adventurer's disclosive space. Now, they're together opening a new one where, let's say, the old American Western attitude of riding into town, doing some good, and then riding away into the sunset is felt as the truly worthy style of feeling and acting. Each listens to words of the other so far as they express and develop this style of feeling and acting. In this way, listening isn't a matter of attaching a meaning to a sound, nor even of attaching a meaning with a whole set of other contextual materials to a sound. *Listening is a matter of attuning oneself to a general style and articulating it by listening to what distinctions are the appropriate ones for this new style.*

The Principle of Articulation

We must dwell on this last point because within it lies the first structuring principle of listening. We want to unpack what's meant by listening to hear which distinctions are the appropriate ones for the mood and style of the current disclosive space being explored, because there's a counterintuitive notion here that we want to get at right away. Don't we just listen to another's words and sentences, we want to ask? What is this "listening for appropriate distinctions"?

These questions exhibit our information-processing view—again, getting in front of our actual way of dealing with people and speaking. To see the way around this, think for a moment of what happens when we read a novel or some other long book. We may carefully read each and every sentence, but we certainly don't respond to each and every sentence. Generally, we don't remember particular sentences. Instead, we build a story or account of our own out of the story we're reading. If we're poor readers or just tired or reading to be entertained, our reading (or listening) focuses on those moments that flesh out or give substance to our normal, highly prized models for handling or seeing things. So, for instance, if we see life—as many do—as a series of tests of our animal cunning that force us to hide our true feelings, then that moment in a story where one character breaks down and tells another that he loves her will be one that we remember, and that we'll use to understand what's already been said. And we'll generally recall all of that material that led us to anticipate that a moment would come where true love was announced.

If, on the other hand, we're like philosophers always waiting to get what the argument is precisely, another moment—one, say, where the lead character says, "You didn't really believe me when I said I loved you, did you?"—will be a moment where this philosophic reader hears the liar's paradox (where nothing said may be believed; even the claim "nothing said may be believed" may be believed). He'll remember the story in terms of those moments, those crucial scenes that make distinctions that fit with a liar's paradox. So while the first reader will read along remembering those scenes that produce distinctions—like the open, loving genuineness of childhood vs. adult scheming, tears and laughter vs. calculative speaking, etc.—the philosophic reader will develop an account and a memory where distinctions suitable to his account are developed. For instance, he'll remember scenes where a genuine childlike openness shades into something humiliating or where a simple tear or laugh seems a betrayal in some obscure way.

Superior, more alert, or more serious readers will try to hold on to those unexpected moments that don't agree with their predisposed ways of listening. These readers will build a relationship with the writer that's meant to change them, rather than merely confirm their predispositions. This kind of reading is one where odd scenes and peculiar, unexpected, and even dry scenes are focused on and recalled again and again until the distinctions implicit in them come out, and a view of things different from the listener's habitual one begins to unfold. This process takes intellectual courage and a professional reader's persistence.

But here's where a salesperson is most like an academic or professional reader. To see this, let's imagine what happens when a real estate agent works with a young couple in helping them find a first home. We can't imagine just any young couple, so let's imagine an urban, apartment-dwelling couple buying their first home, where they can afford it: in the suburbs. When the real estate agent meets them, they're accustomed to all the refinements in life that their low rent has afforded them. They drink fine wines, purchase groceries in gourmet shops. So they tell the real estate agent that they want to be near a grocery store that has arugula and Belgian endive; they also need a wine shop and gourmet coffee store nearby. They know that they'll have to cut back a little, so they say the opera subscription will go, and so will the late stops for decaffeinated cappuccino.

Most of this will sound rather strange to a salesman more accustomed to talking about school quality, the number of children in the neighborhood, the PTA, house design, drainage, yard care, and the rest. But the real estate agent will listen for something he can work with as he builds his relationship with this couple. So in their talking, he notes that they want an older house with some character and hardwood floors. He may not have a very clear idea what "character" or "hardwood floors" means to this couple, but he doesn't simply keep hardwood floors before his mind's eye as a requirement. Instead, it becomes a distinction that he surrounds with other relevant distinctions as he gets a better feel for this couple.

In the meantime, the young couple also find themselves making adjustments. In their conversation with the real estate agent, they begin to notice that neighboring yards are meaningful to them and that yard care is something that they'll have to commit themselves to. They inquire about nurseries, and already, an interest in the finest restaurants seems to shift to an interest in gardening. Again, the real estate agent doesn't hear "closeness to a nursery" as a requirement, but as another charged distinction. As it always is, a relationship is being developed in which the real estate agent is a kind of facilitator from one lifestyle to another. But more than that, the disclosive space that his listening and their listening open up makes them both see things in a new way. He begins to see new aspects of his taken-for-granted suburban setting. Didn't he know before that this grocery store has a wide selection of California, French, and Italian wines while the other has almost exclusively California wines? Well, perhaps, on the very periphery of awareness something like this distinction had occurred to him. But now it's charged; he sees things differently, as they now see yards differently.

The real estate agent begins to see that a particularly styled, shared disclosive space is opening up between him and these customers. They're all starting to see things with an engaged commitment to visual details. And once the salesman gets this, he becomes able to preview houses with his clients in mind and to be able to show them ones that he knows that they'll be interested in. He's even able to present them with new distinctions that fit the way of seeing that they're developing together. This house, he points out, is near a beautiful running track that they could use to keep in shape. And that aspect might more than counter the fact that the nearest nursery is some miles away or that the previous owners didn't care about the hardwood floor and painted without any floor covering because they put wall-to-wall carpets over the whole surface. The agent and the couple know that this could very well be the house the clients purchase.

Now to see what's happened, we need to ask, what if the real estate agent had said, on his first meeting with his clients, that they should be seriously interested in this house because of the nearby running track with beautiful views? This claim would have fallen on deaf ears. The griminess of the city was fine for running, they would've said. A track with beautiful views would have had nothing to do with their "requirements," they might've said. The point is that in their relationship with the salesman, they came to develop a way of seeing the suburbs and their lives there, a way of seeing, that is, which neither one of them had had before. They did this by discovering a new set of charged distinctions that the representative of suburban living — the real estate agent — could make some sense of and that the city dwellers who would move to the suburbs could also make sense of. Note, too, that the distinctions never were completely precise; they were always tentative, to be worked out in actually living in the suburbs.

What makes the real estate agent particularly effective in this situation is that he doesn't simply listen to hear the distinctions that fit his predispositions of how houses in the suburbs *should be* viewed. Nor does he listen to get a precise sense of what this city-dwelling couple means by each of its distinctions. He doesn't try to unpack the strangeness of their concerns by spending, let's say, a couple of days living in the city or by taking a course on what it is like to be an urban yuppie. All he would learn from such an experience or course is why the couple had resisted purchasing a house in the suburbs earlier and why it still seemed something of an unpleasant prospect. Instead, what he did was find one of their charged distinctions to which he could respond—hardwood floors vs. wall-to-wall carpeting— and built from there. He always listened to hear what the tendency or style or pattern or family connection was that organized the charged distinctions that were being developed over the course of their house-hunting together. In this, he wasn't listening to each word or each sentence, but *his listening was attending to the story that was being told by their very interactions together*. He was listening to the distinctions that this interaction was in the course of generating.

The Principle of Collaboration

So *the first structuring principle of listening is attending to the charged distinctions generated in the course of the mutual experience, the shared disclosive space.* The second structuring principle can be seen by thinking about what seems to be a peculiar accident of the account just given of the real estate agent. Surely, we want to say, any number of relationships or disclosive spaces could've come out of the talk and house-hunting expeditions between the agent and this urban couple. How did it work out—or how did the agent make it work out—that the disclosive space developed or that the distinctions he fastened on would lead to their purchasing a house? What kept them, say, from simply becoming good friends or simply people who had, like two passengers on a train, some interesting conversations with each other? *The second structuring feature of good listening is that it attends to distinctions that draw out or draw upon or collect as rich as possible a deposit of skills and aptitudes in the other.*

128

To get at what this principle or even dimension of activity looks and feels like, it's helpful to begin with its absence, which we almost always note right away. Sometimes we'll find ourselves talking to someone who seems to be steering the conversation in one way or another to get a predetermined response. Poor salesmen are notorious for this practice. "Do you want a better life for your children?" an encyclopedia salesman might begin by asking. Or, from a computer company representative to a car rental senior executive, "What if you could reprice your entire fleet of cars moment to moment and redeploy it hourly to fit changing market needs?" Even questions like, "How can my company help you make your vision a reality?" reveal a set agenda and a manipulative stance. Whatever answer is given to those questions, it doesn't go toward developing or exploring a particular disclosive space. Most of all, it doesn't seek to draw out the richest element of the answerer's vision, skills, or practices. At best, the question resounds with the sense that the selling company helped someone else similar to the customer's company and wants to parlay that worked-for sale into a quick profit with this new customer company. Imagine the real estate agent asking the young couple, "What if I could offer you a house in a neighborhood that had all the comforts of the city and all the benefits of the suburbs and offer it to you at a price you could afford?" If we were friends of this couple, our advice would be to run. This real estate sales agent is selling strictly to types, and telling them what he knows they want to hear. This is barren and demeaning.

So if this is the negative experience of the principle of collection, what is its positive counterpart? Let's start out by thinking about our experiences at parties. When we go to parties, whether they include old acquaintances or new people, we find ourselves having long, rewarding conversations with some and brief, unrewarding conversations with others. In fact, the social path we travel is guided by these conversations. We tend to seek the rewarding ones and avoid the unrewarding ones. But how do we mark the difference?

Well, on the one hand, there are those people who are impressed with something we do. They want to hear all about it, and they'll just soak it all in, making appreciative noises now and then. These people weary us. There are also those who are interested in what we do, but they've already pigeonholed or typecast us, so they want to hear us fulfill their expectations. We flee them, too.

What happens when we hit it off with someone? Normally, such people interest us because they take what we've said and try to apply it to their lives and then ask us if this application makes sense. If we sense that the part of their lives to which they've applied our claim is one that they're passionate about, then we find ourselves drawn in. We want to know what we can add to this passionately lived life and what the activities or account of that life can say to us. This isn't to say that we want information or that we want to become a sponge ourselves. Instead, *we find ourselves already in a new, particularly shaped disclosive space that draws on what we both already care about.*

It's very easy to be led astray with this aspect of what happens in such a conversation, because each person will ask the other many particular, concrete questions about what he does. So it could look like each is trying to understand as clearly as possible how the other's practices work. But this would be missing the point. *Each is interested in the other's practice so far as it contributes to the new way of looking at his or her own practices.* Look back to the conversation of the two men in the railroad car. The relief worker doesn't want to know precisely what it's like to be an adventurer; nor does the adventurer want to know precisely what it's like to be a relief worker. But they both want to draw the other out as deeply as possible, in order to get each other to fill out as richly as possible the new disclosive space based on the Western-movie-hero ethos of riding into town doing some good and then riding out. Each will question the other about details of his account to draw out distinctions that aid in developing this ethos. That, too, is what the conversation at the party will do. In short, *each listens to become a literary collaborator with the other.*

But this may all seem too literary. What about the real life of buying and selling things that companies need? Doesn't the activity of collecting there amount to collecting information about what the customer really needs for his business or life and then showing him how a particular product comes closest to fulfilling those needs?

Let's look at selling a car, because if any industry seems to offend in collaboration, it's the car-selling industry. Advertising for cars seems mostly developed to appeal to particular types of people—usually men, either rugged or successful, in various ways. And since prices are fixed by negotiation, animal cunning and manipulation seem to play strong roles. None of these claims can be denied.

But how is it that a person settles on one particular type of car? Let's begin by facing the fact that none of us is immune from all the advertising we see, read, and hear. On the basis of that, our price range, and some rough sense of our needs—How roomy must the car be? How much can we afford for gas? What kinds of materials will we carry in it? Who will see it and evaluate us in terms of it?—we find ourselves presented with a fairly long list of possibilities. But what happens as we go from showroom to showroom? While keeping our basic needs in mind, we nevertheless see purchasing a new car as making a change in our lives; in fact, we probably think of it as making a change in our image. And as we sit in the car, test drive it, pull it up to the curb, and so on, we watch and listen to ourselves, and we listen to others to try to come to terms with the new possible selves we may become. "This car is famous for its high-speed cornering," the salesperson encourages us as we drive on twisty, hilly roads, and so we imagine our future selves taking pleasure in the vehicle's pure speed and control. We see if there's a rich vein in us that wants to treat driving as skiing, and, with his patter, the salesman tries to mine that vein. He gives us new terms for thinking of it and for seeing ourselves in its terms.

Another car promises a smooth, quiet ride; it speaks of success and luxury and we're encouraged to think of the confidence it will inspire in our clients and in ourselves, the ease with which we can conduct business in this car, the way in which the car itself is something to start talking about: its craftsmanship, its security, its luxuriousness.

And so it goes, each ride and each salesman trying to bring out in us the richest experience he possibly can. Which car taps into some raw, untapped, unarticulated resource? That's the question. The car we buy isn't the one that just meets our needs—we can probably find many that do that. The car we buy is the one that makes us feel that there's a rich new sense of ourselves that's already there and is ready to come out. The salesman who's best in collaborating with us in bringing out this richness is generally the one who succeeds in making us buy the car he's selling. And he'll do this only if he himself is passionately committed to listening to the way that the capacities of the car he's selling solicit various excitements and interests in his customers.

In fact, here we may see the principle of collaboration at work most clearly, because the good car salesman will be passionately interested in picking up from all his potential customers ways of working out various responses provoked by his car. His selling is really a kind of teaching; he's teaching his customer how best to draw out what already responds to the car. And the salesman learns this by experience with many different customers fashioning their own sense of themselves in the car. For this salesman, each test drive—even if it doesn't result in a sale—is something to get excited about because of the chance to collaborate with someone on developing his or her image. *Because the car that appeals to some rich sense of ourselves is the one we'll buy.*

So the answer to the question that we began this section with turns out to be quite simple. What is it that will keep a car or real estate salesman in the business of selling cars or real estate if she starts out by trying to build a relationship with a potential customer? The answer has to be because that sales professional develops an understanding of herself through the different kind of life a new car or a new home could give us. That's what she's most passionate about. That's where the potential client can find the saleswoman's richest resources. That's what's going to keep her in that business.

But surely we must recognize that sales professionals change fields and some remain quite successful despite that. How do we account for them? It's precisely the principle of collection or collaboration that keeps them going; only the resource (the product) by which they're able to draw others and themselves out changes. They could never continue to be good salespeople if they didn't allow themselves to be drawn out in terms of the new product they're selling. In fact, some sales professionals thrive from making changes from one product to another.

The Principle of Anomalies

So far this account of listening has made some counterintuitive claims, but has been able to back them up by focusing on the rather average, everyday experiences of having conversations at parties or of purchasing cars and houses, even reading books. On these occasions, we feel that the relationship that occurs between the parties to the event is one where a new relationship is developed, where new capacities are drawn out, and where the more the new relationship or the new possibility reverberates or has effects on our other older relationships and older ways of doing things, the better. We could summarize this by saying that *the principle of articulation produces wonder in us, and the principle of collaboration produces a sense of resonance*.

Now we must get at a third principle of listening that drives the other two; it's peculiar for us that it often drives the other two by its neglect. This neglect shows up most markedly in business sales when the market changes and the sales force and the company strategists have nothing much to say about it—when they're blindsided, so to speak. This happens because they haven't been listening. Although they may have been listening in the ways already described, the clients seem to be deciding that, although they like the relationships they've been building, suddenly they're not relevant anymore; they seem stultifying. The customer feels that he doesn't like what he's becoming anymore. The usual way of saying this in business is that the company's become "too bureaucratic." What has the salesperson not listened to in this case? Where has listening failed?

Usually when we develop a disclosive space with someone, that is, when we develop a relationship, we're so caught up in the wonder and resonance of the new relationship that we attend only to the things that would seem to build it along the lines that made it first click. The two men in the train car will attend to only those aspects of each other's stories that help them both understand their accounts in terms of the old-West ethos. In this, they're listening to something new and not according to their old, ordinary dispositions. They may also be listening to the articulation of the other practices they have that make this very one—of telling stories in the old-West mode—possible. But they're not listening to hear what in each of them also resists this kind of storytelling. We could also say that they're not listening to what, at the margins of their storytelling relationship, drives it along but would have to be articulated along different lines. For instance, they don't hear in their stories a longing that shows up every once in a while in the flatness of an ending for something to change in them so that they don't have to ride off into the sunset, because they have a home to go to. *This sort of listening, a listening for future possibilities and transformations, draws us to recognizing what counter possibilities vex us, and that we push aside, usually without any sense of what we are doing.*

Since this aspect of listening doesn't show up clearly in our average everyday transactions, and since we want to present a fairly pure case of it, we'll have to start by looking at a famous national leader, one whom we may or may not admire. The national leader who manifests a particularly illustrious instance of this principle of listening is Lech Walesa, during the time when he was the mostly underground leader of the Polish Solidarity party. I have no great knowledge of the Polish situation when I say this, just the material presented on National Public Radio. But assuming that such material presents the whole story, then we can see how he listened to more than the obvious solicitations that were being made to him in various disclosive spaces and, how, by listening deeply to what was somewhat anomalous, he created a novel solution to what seemed an intractable problem. The dilemma before him and Solidarity was whether it was worth the loss of life and destitution of the Polish economy to aggressively resist Soviet-backed totalitarianism. According to the Solidarity leaders interviewed on the radio, by and large the party wanted to take control of Poland by means of long-term strikes, work slow-downs, public disobedience, and other similar measures. This thinking was revolutionary and, apparently, more people were being drawn to it. Yet Walesa and many other people realized that this aggressive resistance would likely bring a military response, and even if the resistance succeeded in the end, the country and its economy would be left in a terrible state. But it turns out that Walesa wasn't listening alone to this new attitude of joyful protest with resignation about the long-term results, though he clearly worked with others to develop this new, independent way of thinking. He advanced the articulations of this disclosive space and showed people how it could draw on various rich understandings of themselves because he also heard that what lay under the joyful, yet desperate aggressive resistance was a nervous, earthy love of country and of the Polish people. So while others were genuinely trying to make themselves into revolutionaries, Walesa listened to and developed the nervousness in their speech and imaginings. He did this both among his fellow party members and in his talks with government officials. As he dealt with more people, the nervousness became palpable, and it started driving real negotiation and real compromise. *In listening, then, as attentively to the dominant tone of events as to what resisted this tone, Walesa brought out a possibility that no one suspected was there*. Indeed, Walesa himself couldn't have been sure of it. By and large, it revealed itself in the background of what was more obviously going on. And members of the Solidarity party recount their amazement and even their sense of lost possibilities when Walesa was able successfully to lead negotiations instead of a war.

We're now on the verge of becoming aware of a feature of disclosive spaces to which this third principle of listening is particularly attentive. *Particular disclosive spaces or articulations of disclosive spaces have a tendency to bring about their own end or their own transformation. This is a way of saying that they're never wholly self-contained but always draw upon practices and ways of saying and seeing things that resist them.* Although this may sound a bit obscure or even unlikely, it comes to no more than realizing that a single way of dealing with things just won't work for everything. Our way of dealing with familiar tools won't be a very good way of dealing with the family's best porcelain dishes. And developing any particular relationship with anything, even familiar tools, will eventually open up new possibilities. So simple craftsman's tools eventually opened up possibilities for the sort of large-scale tools in factories that make humans into servants of the industrial system as much as expert manipulators of tools in a single, comprehensible process. One set of practices has other sets of practices implicit within it.

We can see this in a fairly concrete way if we look at the movie industry. If we recall back to the end of the 1960s and the beginnings of the 1970s, many of the famous movies were about small- or big-time crooks and confidence men. Television shows with such types as their lead characters also blossomed. We can see now that these movies and television shows were popular because they expressed dissatisfaction with the way our larger institutions represented us. We felt ourselves frequently to be playing games in which we had no confidence. People too often felt that they were faking it, and these movies and television shows crystallized this for us. But while these movies and television shows articulated a new disclosive space, struck a rich vein within us and gave us a sense of wonder and excitement, they also sensitized us to a vague resistance we had to them. Rather vaguely, we felt that it was wrong to be fake, to be on the outside like an outlaw. And this resistance is precisely what was picked up and articulated by the adventure movies of the early 1980s with their naive confidence and forthrightness. Although this form of expression is still popular with us, these, too, bring out a rather vague resistance in us that tells us that matters are too simple in those movies.

Now a very serious mistake could be made right here: one could think that the deep listening to anomalies just discussed is a way of listening bent on prophesy or analytically projecting the future. This isn't it at all. The point is *that one has to listen to how the anomalous resistance can be articulated*. One listens to this in the same way that the real estate salesman listened to his young couple or the way the reader of a book makes up a story that takes account of what seems like the important distinctions. But in this case, one listens to the reverse side of one's own activity of listening. So instead of simply listening to the young couple, the salesman should listen to what strikes a hollow note in his own listening. "Is it perhaps a little hard to believe that real estate investments are always supposed to be great ways of providing shelter, a tax write-off, and capital appreciation. Shouldn't these three aspects of home-purchasing be unbundled?" In listening to whatever it is that resists the relationship he builds, he'll be articulating a future as well as the present. If he shares his articulations, he'll be making a future.

To make this principle of listening clearer, we need to get a better fix on why we don't normally experience it. What happens when we find our clients resisting what we say or criticizing us? We normally try to handle the resistance or criticism as it stands in terms of our overall relationship. We'll take it as an opportunity to deepen our relationship in the very terms in which we have been developing it. *We fix things*. In this way, we don't ask ourselves if there's another way of seeing things or of treating things that might very well be the source of the resistance or complaint. If we sense that our client's criticism has something more substantial in it, we'll more than likely begin thinking in the information-processing mode and research the client's company, competitive status with other companies in his industry, develop a profile, and determine how to market to this industry type. A major computer company presents a good example of what this sort of activity looks like, and it can also show us what precisely the company misses.

This company was in the habit of inviting the CIOs of its largest clients to a major company event that took place each year just before the Super Bowl. The company would introduce the CIOs to new research, new advances in computer design, and proposed and expected systems, and then the CIOs would be invited to sit in the company box at the Super Bowl. During one of the winding-down sessions, where an officer from the computer company was supposed to summarize the meetings and get some reactions, one CIO said that he was simply wearied by hearing all about the computer company's newest technology, how much faster, more muscle-bound, integrated, and the rest that it was. He wanted the computer company to solve his problems. During the meeting, the officer had little to say in response. But he realized that this remark wasn't just some bit of random dissatisfaction. Instead, he and other people in his company determined that the industry would no longer be technology driven. The industry was transforming itself under their eyes and becoming customer driven. It was at this point that the company determined that its sales force would have to be retrained so that its members could act as consultants to the industries that they served. This way, the company could solve the client's problems and continue to dominate its field. Is there any better case of listening than this? Or is there any worse?

This is precisely a case of being insensitive to the relationship already developed and the ways that it can be renewed. To see this, we should just ask if it's really likely that a CIO would ask the computer company to offer him consultants in addition to their computers. Was this CIO really starved for consultants? In his industry, that's unlikely. Instead, the computer company had developed a relationship with its client companies where it was understood to bring each company outstanding equipment and service. All of this was very high tech. Its technicians were top notch, and if a computer went down, it was quickly back up and working. How could a CIO find any problem with such a cozy relationship? Most likely, the answer has to do with the very success of the relationship, not so much a change in the industry, although an industrywide change might very well have been in the offing.

As the computer company provided faster computers on which more applications could run, the CIO probably found himself facing additional expectations from other division executives and fewer of them could be met by simple or complicated upgrades of one sort or another. Does this mean that he wanted the computer company to figure out ways to solve these problems for him? Or does he want the computer company to start providing him with tools that will help him solve his own problem? Obviously, "want" is too strong a word here; he doesn't want anything in particular. But if we're listening to the resistances correctly, we may suspect that a relationship built on providing tools to help thinking—to support concentration and research—is what he "wants." This doesn't require that the computer company provide consultants, but that they provide the kinds of tools that people in companies full of data need.

Conclusion

Has this essay simply argued for a holistic approach to listening? That is, are we saying that each relationship with each customer has to be taken as unique, and what is said has to be understood strictly in terms of that relationship? The answer to these questions goes in two different directions. And the reason for this is that holism has been misunderstood. If we say, "Yes, each customer relationship must be taken separately, and everything the customer says must be understood in terms of that relationship," then this claim seems right off to be an impossible one to meet. Because how could a business really manage that many different relationships? Does this mean that everything a business sells must be customized for each customer, no matter what? To say yes to this would seem pure nonsense, and that is what holism looks like it demands, some sort of super-human task precisely of the kind the first section of this essay acknowledged to be impossible.

It's part of the holistic understanding that this account promotes that it doesn't require salespeople to become supermen of one sort or another. Instead, this account explains what good salespeople do from the very beginning. They don't learn all they possibly can about other industries. *Good sales professionals become passionately engaged in knowing as much as they can about their own products and look to work with the customer to find ways of making his or her business more productive by using these products.* In short, the home companies' products become a tool for thinking about the way any business works. This doesn't require that salespeople become super humans who can understand dozens of different kinds of businesses. Instead, this essay advocates that they genuinely use their products as tools for thinking about and understanding those businesses they sell to. Just as the good real estate sales agent thinks about her clients in terms of their style of real-estate thinking and selection, so other sales professionals should do the same.

The second change in approach to listening that this essay intends to promote is that *listening isn't about receiving information; listening is about building a rapport*. One doesn't try to get as much information as possible but instead should try to find what critical distinctions both listener and speaker can share and develop. And critical distinctions aren't just the customers concerns about the particular product a salesperson might sell, but they're the distinctions that suggest the way the product will be used and the way future products might also be used. This isn't to say that the salesperson should be passive until he or she hears what benefits the client wants and then go about selling the benefits and delivering the features—the old model of selling. Instead, *the salesperson ought to listen to hear how his product enables him to think about the client's business in a revealing way*. The more revealing, the better. And the resistances are to be taken as seriously as the acceptances, because the future of the relationship lies in these. Because ultimately what the salesman is always selling is a better business practice, one that promises to continuously provide a better way of handling employees, customers, venders, and products.